The Twible

Advance Praise

"*The Twible* adapts the Old Testament to the light-hearted quipping familiar in everyday Tweets."
—*The Guardian*, UK

"*The Twible* is the most entertaining version of my dad's book I've read in the last two millennia!"
—Jesus Christ†

"Twible is the best example I have ever seen of the reverence of irreverence. Only those who love deeply and securely can bring this kind of humor to the telling of the family's stories. Don't read it, unless you are prepared to fall in love with them again."
—Phyllis Tickle, author of *The Divine Hours* and *The Great Emergence*

"I wouldn't object if *Twibles* were in every hotel room. If they're using this book, I look forward to the next time Christians attempt to proselytwize me."
—Hemant Mehta, The Friendly Atheist blogger; author of *The Young Atheist's Survival Guide*

"Forget about reading the Bible in a year. Now you can read it in an hour, thanks to the subversive, somewhat disturbed, mind of Jana Riess. She tweets you through all 1,189 chapters of the Bible, and manages to capture the main point—and often the general weirdness factor—of each chapter. After reading this book, whether you are new to the Bible or a seasoned veteran, you will agree that this woman needs help. But along the way, you'll also get a fresh, funny, and profound take on the Bible you never knew or thought you knew."
—Peter Enns, author of *Genesis for Normal People* and *The Evolution of Adam: What the Bible Does and Doesn't Say about Human Origins*

"The perfect (surreptitious) iPad or Tablet companion for draggy Sunday (or Saturday) morning services. Caution: Not to be used for congregational Scripture reading."
—Mark I. Pinsky, author of *The Gospel According to the Simpsons*

"Whatever you think of Twitter, there can be no speedier or funnier way to read through the Bible than with Riess's *Twible* providing spot-on interpretation chapter by chapter. On a jet stream of solid scholarship, it'll keep you thinking long after the hashtags have burned away."
—Kristin Swenson, author of *Bible Babel: Making Sense of the Most Talked-about Book of All Time*

"*The Twible* is an indelible book that reads like an oddly religious comedy but has the impact of a brilliant jingle that sticks in your brain to the point of madness. Read it and drive yourself pleasantly nuts."
—Frank Schaeffer, author of *And God Said, "Billy!"*

"This is brilliant stuff—hilariously accurate summaries of complex material. I love *The Twible*. I will keep it next to all my stodgy commentaries, not just for a laugh, but because it is imperative, I believe, to approach the Bible with a sense of humor if we hope to understand it. Riess is a very funny, charmingly masterful guide. Everyone should have *The Twible* next to the Bible. It will help you get through the sometimes dense and hoary text—laughing."
—Debbie Blue, pastor; author of *Consider the Birds: A Provocative Guide to the Birds of the Bible*

"This is absolutely the funniest and most fun Bible 'translation' ever. Yet, throughout the ensuing hilarity there is a wisdom here that challenges and provokes. It's hard to get around the fact that while you are having a blast reading Riess's laugh-out-loud redaction of the scriptures, you are often left reflecting on the Biblical verses from a new, and slightly skewed, angle. Like the court jester who exposes the king to troubling and potent truths clothed as cunning jests, this book forced me to reexamine and reinterpret my mundane habits of viewing the text, sometimes in startling ways that both delighted and vexed me out of my safe and comfortable familiarity. Don't miss *The Twible*."
—Steven L. Peck, author of *A Short Stay in Hell* and *The Scholar of Moab*

† This is not actually the Jesus of the New Testament. He was busy and could not be reached for comment. This is that other guy.

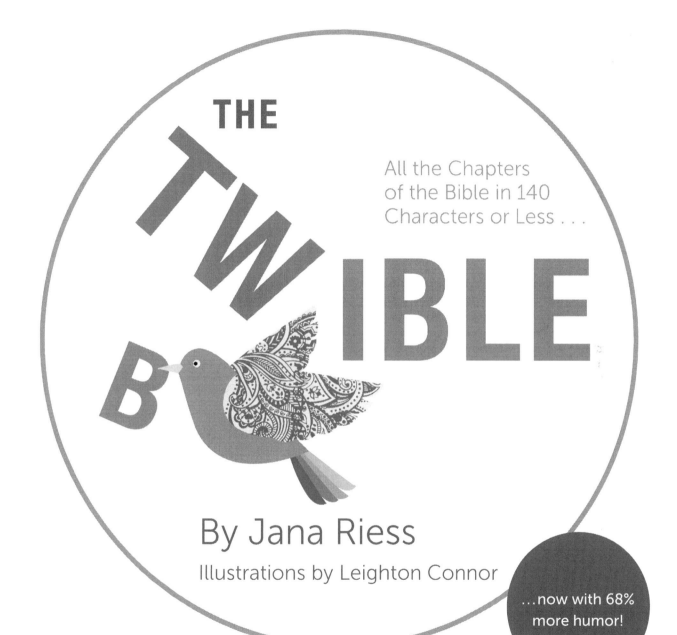

THE TWIBLE

All the Chapters
of the Bible in 140
Characters or Less . . .

By Jana Riess

Illustrations by Leighton Connor

...now with 68%
more humor!

© 2013

ISBN 978-0-9897747-0-3

1st edition

Published by Jana Riess

12 13 14 15 16 17 18 19 20 21 — 10 9 8 7 6 5 4 3 2 1

Scripture quotations from the New Revised Standard Version of the Bible are copyright © 1989 by the Division of Christian Education of the National Council of the Churches of Christ in the U.S.A.

Book design by Paraclete Press
Cover design by Paraclete Press
Illustrations by Leighton Connor

PRINTED IN THE UNITED STATES OF AMERICA

In memory of my beloved mother, Phyllis Riess,

1941-2013

Contents
(Or, Every Book of the Bible Explained in Seven Words or Less. Go.)

Introduction

I love the Bible.

I tell you this now just in case you begin to wonder about my feelings down the road, when you see me railing at God for slaughtering all the Midianites or pointing out how King David's family put the fun in dysfunctional. I have issues with the Bible, sure, but always in the context of a lover's quarrel. And I'm fond enough of the Bible to know that it can take a good-natured joke. Or, in the case of this book, 1,189 of them.

Here's how it started. In the fall of 2009, on a trip to Southern California (the birthplace of more than one bizarre religious idea), I consulted the Bible in my hotel nightstand for a single piece of information. Flipping through its pages I was then struck, Old Testament lightning-style, by how many parts of the Bible I had never read. I could not at that time have told you what an ephod was, or why the Books of Chronicles omit kingly tabloid headlines that were so salacious when the same stories were told in 2 Samuel. And the Book of Habakkuk? No idea.

So I decided to try an experiment: I would work my way through the entire Bible, summarizing a chapter a day on Twitter in 140 characters or less but with humorous commentary. And I would do this *Twible* (rhymes with Bible) project in community. Like many people of faith, I had tried before to read the Bible cover to cover, without success. But through social media I discovered a reading community of people who wanted to know more about the Bible, but could never get very far on their own. Apparently it takes a virtual village to get some people to read the Bible, myself included.

I've learned a great deal I never knew about the Good Book, including the following important facts that are highly relevant to daily life:

- If one of my friends has a dream in which a foreign god speaks to her, I am supposed to kill her on the spot. It is good to know this in advance, as wholesale slaughter can really put a damper on a relationship.

- The Book of Revelation has another nativity story that's not quite like the shepherd-and-manger one from the Gospel of Luke. In this one, a sparkly woman gives birth to baby Jesus with a dragon in attendance so it can get first dibs on eating the baby. It's difficult to pull this off in local Christmas pageants, so the story gets little play.

- When God promised Noah that he would never again destroy the earth by flood, he didn't say anything about the earthquakes and tsunamis he was holding in reserve. So do watch the Weather Channel.

- When God's spirit departs from the Jerusalem temple in the Book of Ezekiel, it's like in *Star Trek* where the Enterprise's shields go down and they're vulnerable to Klingon attack. You really don't want to be on the ship at that moment.

- There are 150 Psalms, which can be five months of your life if you are tweeting the Bible every day. It turns out that is a very long time.

I've also learned that the Bible is a wonderful collection of teachings about God. Its 66 books run the gamut from God as Punisher-in-Chief (Numbers) to God as a merciful and loving Dad who just can't understand why his kids give him crap all day long (Hosea). Its characters are schemers and prophets, failures and heroes, lovers and fighters—and all those contradictions can be embodied in the same individual. (I'm talking to you, Jacob.)

In short, the Bible is wildly complicated. *The Twible*, by contrast, is pretty simple. Its goal is to make you laugh. If you learn something along the way, as I have, all the better. It's certainly true that most of us, even those who identify ourselves as Jewish or Christian, don't know a lot about the Bible these days. Gallup polls suggest that "basic Bible reading is at a record low," and religion scholar Stephen Prothero cites surveys showing that although two-thirds of Americans think that the Bible has the answers to life's most important questions, they're not actually reading it. Most cannot name the first book of the Bible; only half can identify even one of the four Gospels; and ten percent think that Joan of Arc is Noah's wife. (That last bit is not a joke, unfortunately, even though it sounds exactly like something *The Twible* would make up.)

As I've been tweeting the Bible, the greatest compliment I've received is when people thought something was funny. One woman told me that a morning tweet was amusing enough that she snorted coffee out her nose, which made my day because causing readers to spew beverages should be the express goal of every writer. The main purpose of this project has always been to bring levity to an all-too-serious subject. But the second-greatest compliment I've gotten is when people tell me that *The Twible* has actually sent them to the original Bible to see for themselves what these stories have to say.

You can read *The Twible* any way you please. You might do it straight through from Genesis to Revelation so that you can brag to your friends and kids that yes, of course you have read the entire Bible and you know exactly what the book of Obadiah is about. (It's about killing Edomites, since you asked.) Or maybe you will read *The Twible* just for the cartoons. There are more than fifty of them in this book, because how fun is the Bible without cartoons? It's fine if you want to laugh at the pictures instead of reading the text. That's how I read *The New Yorker*, only don't tell anybody.

You'll see throughout the book that some biblical characters' names have been shortened for Twitter usage. God goes by G, Jesus is JC, and Job is just Job, because poor Job loses so many other things in the Bible that it seemed like the final insult to also abbreviate the letters in his name. If you ever get confused about who's who, just check out the glossary at the back of the book.

The Bible says that a cheerful heart is good medicine (Prov. 17:22), so it's my hope that *The Twible* contributes to a cheerful heart and therefore to your overall health. Happy reading.

Jana

Hebrew Bible

Old Testament

GENESIS

Overview: In the beginning were some messed-up folks and a God who couldn't decide whether to love them or kill them. Say amen.

1: After 6 days of creation, G's totally wiped. Day off tomorrow! Key point: human beings very good. M and F in G's image.

2: 2nd creation story. G forms Adam from dust; very green, 100% recycled material. Eden good. Don't eat *that* tree. Yep, that one.

3: Adam and Eve social climbers. Drink antioxidants from pomegranate juice so as to live forever. Doesn't work out; G's ticked. Exile.

4: Adam and Eve find sex fun, but kids are a problem. Cain forgets meds; offs Abel. "Am I my bro's keeper?" Abel replaced with Seth. Ouch.

Two By Two By Seven

You know all those songs about how Noah brings one pair of each animal onto the arky, arky? Well, if you were an unclean animal, that's a totally accurate picture. Mr. and Mrs. Pig, for example, would both happily lumber onto the boat that would save their entire piggy race. So it would go for the unclean.

But if you were a clean animal (lucky you!), Noah was supposed to bring along seven pairs of you. Was he saving all seven because they were special, you ask? Good question. But no. The Bible isn't as sweet as all that. The other pairs of clean animals were destined for sacrifice.

(Just as an early FYI, a *lot* of the creatures and people you meet in this book are going to die. It's a Bible thing.)

5: Adam dies @ 930 years. It's all downhill from here as life span dwindles. Except for Methuselah @ 969 years. He ate whole grains.

6: Nephilim demigods get it on with human chicks and sire giants. Weirdest passage in Torah? G has maker's remorse and regrets humanity.

7: Weather alert! G gives Noah 1 week eviction notice: "Take 7 pairs of each clean animal in Ark to avoid flood. Oh, and BYO Renuzit."

8: After 190+ days, H2O subsides. However, a crummy vacation package requires 150 more days of waiting on the stinky ship for FEMA cleanup.

9: They've de-arked. G sends a rainbow to promise he'll never again murder us by flood. Keeps earthquakes, tsunamis & hurricanes in reserve.

10: Begat, begat, begat. Name index includes Ludium, Lehabim and Jerah, all now available by prescription. Ask your doctor about Ophir.

11: We built this city! We built this city on rock and stone! Bad idea; G annoyed. Language scattered. *No puedo entenderte.*

12: Hello, Abram. G promises land and descendants. Father Ab responds by lying to Pharaoh and pimping out wife Sarai. What a bright future.

13: Abram, loaded with cash, divides turf with nephew Lot. Lot gets Sodom, a risky real estate investment. Be sure to buy fire insurance.

14: Four kings seize Lot. Oh no! Ab comes to the rescue even though Lot's the village idiot. Maybe blood really is thicker than water.

God's Plan B

"The first eleven chapters [of Genesis] . . . are about the relationship between God and the entire human community. That relationship does not go well, and after ten generations the deity decides to destroy the mass and start over with a single virtuous man's family [Noah]. But it turns out that choosing a virtuous individual does not guarantee that this individual's descendents will be virtuous as well. Another ten generations pass, and humans in general are not a planet-full of Noahs. So once again the focus narrows to a single virtuous person, Abraham. We must keep in mind what has happened up to this point when we read this, or else we will lose the significance of what is happening here. Wiping out everyone but a virtuous person did not work. So God leaves the species alive but chooses an individual who will produce a family that will ultimately bring blessing to all the families of the earth."

■ Richard Elliott Friedman, *Commentary on the Torah*

15: Ab: "Where's that friggin' heir you promised?" G: "Number the stars. So will your offspring be. You're gonna need a bigger boat."

16: Barren Sarai begs Ab to bed down with slave girl Hagar. This solution spawns a son but also impressive catfights. Ab gets a migraine.

17: Abram now Abraham. G was clearly not thinking ahead about the Twitter character count. Name longer; foreskin snipped. A tradeoff.

18: *The Negotiator.* Ab: "What if 50 righteous are in Sodom?" G: "OK, I won't torch if I find 50." Ab: "45? 40? 30? 10?" G: "OK, OK! Lay off!"

19: Lot sacrifices his own daughters to the raping hordes. BTW, Lot's the GOOD guy in chapter 19. Just in case you were wondering.

20: Ab pulls the "she's my sister" act again; successfully pimps out Sarah for more sheep, oxen, and slaves. Three cheers for Father Ab!

21: Ab (100) and Sarah (90) have Isaac without IVF. Wow! But they don't need Hagar anymore, so they throw her under a passing bus.

22: Ultimate psych test: G commands sacrifice of Ab's chosen son Isaac. Ram saves day @ the last minute. Um, what kind of G is this?

The Top Five Incestuous Relationships in Genesis

1. Judah sleeping with daughter-in-law Tamar (Gen. 38). FYI: Judah actually mistakes her for an anonymous prostitute, which would of course make everything morally above board. So stop your judging.

2. Cain and whoever he had kids with (Gen. 4). If you interpret the Bible literally and believe that Adam and Eve were the first people on the earth, his mate had to be his own dear sister, because she would have been almost the only game in town at that point. The other option would be Eve, Cain's mom, but let's not even go there.

3. Lot and his daughters (Gen. 19). Lot's two daughters get him drunk and seduce him, then nine months later bear Ammon and Moab, respectively. And this from the people who were righteous enough to survive Sodom and Gomorrah.

4. Sarah and Abraham (Gen. 20). They're half-siblings, so when Abraham excuses his behavior of prostituting Sarah to wealthy men with the "she's my sister" routine, he's actually half-right.

5. Reuben and Bilhah (Gen. 35). Jacob's son Reuben has an affair with Jacob's concubine Bilhah, the mom of Dan and Naphtali. And there is Reuben wondering why he isn't Dad's favorite child. Hmmm.

Sibling Rivalry in the Bible

You know the Bible's going to be a brother-on-brother kind of book right from the beginning, when Cain slays Abel. Never mind that Abel was kind of a suckup who might have deserved it, or that God is patently unfair to Cain. It's still fratricide.

The rivalry of Jacob and Esau sets a pattern in the Bible for younger brothers to subvert the whole primogeniture thing and put themselves forward. Jacob may trail Esau in coming out of the womb, but he's top of the class in deceit, tricking their dad (and Esau, who comes across as a bit of an oaf) into giving him the blessings and rights that should have been Esau's. Nicely played, Jacob.

But turnabout is fair play in the Bible, and Jacob soon watches with horror as similar dramas unfold among his own twelve sons. Next-to-youngest son Joseph has big dreams and his father's unswerving devotion, so he's Public Enemy Number One in the eyes of his older brothers. First they try to kill him but then decide merely to sell him into slavery and lie to Dad about it.

It's not like the younger brother pattern stops with Genesis. In Exodus, we'll see Moses become more important than Aaron; later, wimpy runt David surpasses all his older brothers to be chosen as the next king; and later still, David's semi-bastard Solomon takes the throne when his older brothers try to kill Dad and each other.

How's that for family values?

23: Sarah dies at 127 and Ab nabs choice burial plot. (This chapter is mostly filler after the drama of the-sacrifice-that-wasn't. Yawn.)

24: Meet-cute 1. Isaac is told, "Whoever waters the camels is your girl." Rebecca wins! See tabloids for spicy details & glam wedding pics.

25: Reb's twins have a WWF-worthy prenatal throwdown. (Psst! Foreshadowing.) Esau's 1stborn, but Jake's a real trickster. Watch your back.

26: Like father, like son. Isaac mimics the "she's my sister" act to pimp out wife Reb. Again leads to riches. We never learn.

27: Jake tricks Isaac into blessing him instead of big brother Esau. Isaac, like Brad Pitt, appears to have facial recognition challenges.

28: Jake gets outta Dodge but suffers weird ladder-climbing dreams. This "stone for a pillow" stuff is a far cry from Westin's Heavenly Bed.

29: Meet-cute 2. Jake works 24/7 to wed Rachel, but her dad pulls a sneaky switch and substitutes Leah instead. Way to trick the trickster.

30: Rach to G: "Gimme kids!" Finally, Rach has Joseph, one of Jake's 11 (later 12) sons. There's also a daughter, or 6, or possibly 21.

31: Rach steals family idols and sits on them. Says she's having red tent issues, but Jake's the one who acts like he's got PMS.

32: Jake wrestles with an angel. Man, he'll pick fights with *any*body! Moral: when you want G's blessing, always employ violence.

33: Jake and Esau reconcile. Well, sort of. "Let's do lunch," says Jake, while settling his family a REALLY safe distance away.

34: Rape of Dinah. Jake arranges a shotgun wedding, but the bros prefer vigilante justice. Blood, gore. Your typical day in Bibleland.

35: Jake purifies the house of all foreign idols, but Rach dies in childbirth anyway. Such is G's loyalty rewards program.

36: Footnote. Esau is the father of the Edomites. They don't become important until the Book of Obadiah, or maybe ever. Begat, begat.

37: 11 Bros ticked when Joseph dreams of lording it over them. First they deep-six him in a pit, then try human trafficking. Joe enslaved. ☹

38: Trouble back home. Judah's ex-DIL Tamar asserts her rights, dressing as a whore to nab Judah as her new hubby. Um, eeeeew.

"Joseph's coat annoyed his brothers..."

39: Joe's a model slave until he's falsely accused of a sex scandal with the boss's wife. So then he's sold down the Nile. Literally.

40: Joe interprets the dreams of a cupbearer ("Early parole!") and a baker ("You're wearing a very red shirt"). Chef, you've been chopped.

41: Joe interprets Pharaoh's funky dream about feast & famine; supervises massive Agriculture program. Joe's a hero & leader. A bit smarmy.

42: Meanwhile, back at the ranch in Canaan, Joe's family begins to starve. So they trek to Egypt for food stamps in hieroglyphics.

43: The brothers are so wigged out w/ hunger that they don't recognize Joe, who's oddly glad to see his would-be murderers. Family ties.

44: Still no Big Reveal. Joe frames Ben as thief to test his brothers' family values. They pass when Judah offers himself instead. A+.

45: FINALLY the teary reunion. Joe forgives his brothers and sets whole family up for life. *Extreme Makeover: OT Edition.* Robes, gifts.

46: G persuades an aging Jake to move the entire clan to Egypt. It's not like there's a single twig left to eat in Canaan anyway.

47: Phar nationalizes land and livestock. He also begins to enslave people, a policy that will bite him in the ass in about 400 years.

48: History repeats itself when Jake swaps the deathbed blessings of his grandsons, favoring younger bro Ephraim. A trickster to the end.

49: Dying Jake chastises Reuben and praises Judah. (How soon we forget Tamargate.) The 12 brothers are now the 12 tribes of Israel.

50: Bros to Joe: "No hard feelings?" Joe: "Nah, we're square. It's super that you tried to kill and enslave me. I so totally love you guys!"

Twible Tip to Straighten Out the Genesis Patriarchs

If you're having trouble remembering all five generations, use alphabetical order for each major patriarch: Abraham, Isaac, Jacob, Joseph, and Manasseh.

This technique doesn't work with the women's names, but women appear to be afterthoughts anyway, so, you know, whatever.

EXODUS

Overview: Exodus tells of slavery to freedom, idolatry to covenant. Also, Egypt gets some utterly craptastic plagues. Karma much?

1: Egyptians freak out about immigrants and enslave all Hebrews. Nasty Phar wants firstborn Heb sons killed, but refusenik midwives rebel.

2: Baby Moses: "I'm cool with floating down the Nile in a basket, but who is this Egyptian chick I'm supposed to call Mom?"

3: Moses is married! (Wasn't it just in chapter 2 that he was a baby?). G (aka "I AM") appears in a burning bush and frets about Heb slaves.

4: Zippy performs ad hoc circumcision on her husband Mo. And did we mention she does this because G's trying to kill him? Um, WHAT?

5: Bipolar G recovers from manic episode to help Mo present iconic "Let my people go!" speech to hardhearted Phar. But . . . EPIC FAIL.

6: [We interrupt this story to bring you Mo and Aaron's Hebrew creds. Also, G claims to have a viable exit strategy from Egypt.]

7: G gets serious, turning the Nile and all water to blood. But G also gives Phar ODD so he won't budge. Talk about your cross-purposes.

8: Frogs and gnats and flies, oh my! Phar promises to let Hebs have a few days off, but then reneges. *Horrible Bosses* indeed.

9: Pestilence, boils, and hail. G's not playing around with wee gnats anymore. But why does G harden Phar's heart? Why not end it now?

Let My People Go . . . On Vacation

In the movie *The Ten Commandments*, Charlton Heston uses a dramatic "Let my people go!" speech to get Pharaoh to free all the slaves. So that must be right, right?

Maybe not exactly. In the Bible, all that Moses has officially asked for up to this point is a few days off. Just a few lousy vacation days so that the Hebrews can go to the wilderness and make a sacrifice to this pesky new God who keeps bugging the hell out of Moses. (See Ex. 5:1 and 8:25-28.)

But Pharaoh wasn't born yesterday, and he probably realizes that the proposed "vacation" is in fact a planned defection, even if the text is pretty coy about it. So he says no. Again and again and again. And as is often the case with revolutions, what might have started out as a request for a simple concession from a superpower becomes in the end a full-blown revolt with kajillions of frogs thrown in for good measure.

Did the Exodus Really Happen?

Good question. Here's one scholar's take on it.

"As with the preceding book of Genesis, and as will continue to be the case until well in 1 Kings, there is no direct link between the persons and events described in Exodus 1-15 and nonbiblical sources. In the abundant texts from ancient Egypt, there is no mention of Moses or Aaron, nor of plagues, nor a killing of the firstborn, nor the drowning of Pharaoh's army. Now absence of evidence is not, as Carl Sagan put it, evidence of absence, and it is at least possible that, as is often true of the ancient Egyptians and other powers throughout history, defeats were simply not recorded. But there is no evidence."

■ Michael Coogan, Director of Publications for the Harvard Semitic Museum, in *The Old Testament: A Very Short Introduction*

10: G tells Mo that he's made Phar obstinate so there'll be a more dramatic Seder for the grandkids later. There's always that explanation.

11: Phar, don't say you weren't warned: all firstborn sons in Egypt will be toast unless you FINALLY give up. Which (spoiler) you won't.

12: G debuts cooking show with only unleavened ingredients. Heb viewers follow tips & save their firstborns! But Egyptians don't have cable.

13: Don't let the door hit you on the way out, Israel. Keep up the unleavened bread thing. Wait, is that Phar on your trail? Step on it!

14: Phar pursues Israel across Red Sea while monologuing. Then G drowns the Egyptians, because not enough people have died yet in Exodus.

15: Miriam's song. Oldest oral tradition in entire Bible? "Our God Is an Awesome God" for the *1200 BCE WOW Gold Hits Album.* Now on iTunes.

16: Exodusters grumble, grumble. G sends manna (literally: "What is it?") 6 of 7 days. Honey Grahams in the wilderness, water from the rock.

17: Isr: "Manna sucks. We miss Egypt. Waaaaah!" You can take the people out of slavery, but you can't take slavery out of the people.

18: FIL Jethro offers burned-out apprentice Mo sound leadership advice about delegating responsibility. Not bad for a godless Midianite.

19: G gives Israel a holy pep talk, then says the people aren't allowed to touch Mt. Sinai. Or have sex. This is some serious tough love.

Is God Trustworthy?

"The people are never really sure about what's going to happen next. They seem scared and nervous. What about water? What about food? I don't blame them at all . . . Sometimes they get a reputation for being whiners, but I can only imagine that I would be worse.

This 'God' led them out of Egypt, but they don't trust him yet—they didn't really know him that well. He (if 'he' is even a very good way of putting it) is a bit enigmatic, after all. Who can blame them? Will God provide for what they need now? There was a dramatic delivery, but what about sustenance? How is this God going to behave in the day-to-day? It's one thing to part water and do miraculous big hero-type things; it's another to provide sustenance. And why wouldn't there be an underlying suspicion of the god of the violent and the dramatic delivery? This God sent a plague that killed little Egyptian babies. There might be reasons not to trust a god that behaves like that."

■ Debbie Blue, *Consider the Birds*

20: G's Top 10 List. No gods, idols, or blasphemy. Keep the Sabbath holy & love Mom. Don't kill, cheat, steal, lie, or look @ Xmas catalogs.

21: Sheriff G lays down the law about murder, punishment, and property disputes. Don't let your oxen roam free. It rarely ends well.

22: Sheriff G orders Israel to be nice to aliens because A) Isr was once the outcast, and B) any alien might actually be Dr. Who. Or Alf.

23: Don't stomp on the poor; do take every seventh year off. (Seriously. A whole year.) Thou shalt not eat bacon double cheeseburgers.

24: G lures Mo to Sinai mountaintop timeshare retreat for 40 days by promising stone tablets to take home after G's spiel. And a free iPad.

25: Giving specs for the Not-Yet-Lost Ark, G's surprisingly micromanagerial about architectural detail. Mercy seat, table, lampstand. Check.

26: G gets seriously overinvolved in blueprints for Tabernacle. Hires HGTV designer to ensure purple and crimson drapes will "pop."

27: G orders Tab interior design: "Top of the line, all the way! Courtyard, lighting, artwork, and maybe a stainless steel kosher kitchen."

Argumentative Conversations with God

The story of the Golden Calf is an odd one. The people become anxious because Moses is AWOL, communing on some mountaintop with God while they're stuck down below trying to figure out daily life in this new wilderness. Will Moses ever come back? What is taking so long? Who's in charge? Who moved their cheese?

So they go to Aaron and demand that he make a god for them, an idol they can worship. Doing so makes them feel more secure. Having a lovely giant gold cow they can see and touch seems a lot more reassuringly predictable than this strange new deity who shouts from a cloud and tried to kill Moses that one time (Ex. 4).

Ironically, Moses is, right at that very moment, defending the people to God. God tells him that the people have become corrupted in Moses' absence and have fashioned an idol for themselves. God's pretty sick of the Israelites, to tell the truth. He tells Moses to go away so he can smite the people in peace and have done with it.

God doesn't get what he wants, though, because Moses turns out to be a skilled defense attorney. He builds quite a case for the Israelites: God's got an Abrahamic covenant to uphold, after all. And besides, it's going to be hugely embarrassing if God went to all the trouble of saving the Israelites from Egypt only to murder them himself five minutes later. Think of the scandal. All the other gods would be talking about it.

So God relents. I find this about-face interesting, because I do a fair amount of arguing with God myself. I like it when the characters in the Bible stand up to God and God takes them seriously. I am the sort of person who believes that God can take a little pushback.

Apparently there's a rabbinic tradition that feels this way too. In *The Particulars of Rapture*, Torah scholar Avivah Gottlieb Zornberg says that some commentators have upheld Moses as a hero for going toe-to-toe with God and refusing to allow him to destroy the world. And you know who Moses' foil is in all this? Noah. That's right; the Genesis patriarch we think of as being so righteous can also be viewed as condoning a holocaust. These interpreters see "Noah's obedience to God's commands—to build the ark and save his own family as a genetic basis for a future humanity" as inhumane; "what looks like normative obedience is in fact collusion in the destruction of the world."

Bottom line: when God tells Noah that he's going to annihilate 99.9% of the world's people and animals, Noah doesn't bat an eyelash. He is all about the coming genocide. When God tells Moses that he's going to wipe out just a fraction of that number, Moses argues for each life like it's his own.

Go Moses!

28: *Priests' Project Runway!* G turns from interior design to fashion. Ephod's hottest garment since the loincloth. Blue's your color, Isr.

29: How-to for priests' ordination: 1 bull, 2 rams, lots o' blood. Get blood on Aar's right ear. Wash ephod in Tide on delicate cycle.

30: A voluntary—er, we mean mandatory—offering is assessed to pay for G's decorating spree. A plague be upon those who don't pay!

31: G feels sorry for Bezalel and Oholiab because of their names, so he hires them for HGTV. Threatens death penalty for Sabbath rebels.

32: Isr: "This new god's OK, but what we really need is a nice golden calf. Idolatry's *way* more fun than this monotheism schtick."

33: G commands Israel to go to Canaan and promises to attend to the minor matter that there are already other people living there.

34: Once more, with feeling! G has Mo do the two tablets all over again. G insists he is slow to anger. Well, except that one time.

35: Wanted: donations for new Tabernacle. G favors gold but will accept gems. Or any other treasure you're willing to cough up.

36: People are so generous with offerings for the Tabernacle that G declares a moratorium on crocheted doilies. No more!

37: The *Ask This Old Ark* crew reveals proper carpentry techniques for mercy seat and other décor. Cherubim carving is especially tricky.

38: No altar's complete without a spot to grill your best animals for G, who prefers teriyaki sauce but will accept mesquite in a pinch.

39: G keeps the Tabernacle construction project debt-free by being his own general contractor. He likes to give the orders, our G.

40: Voilà! Tabernacle & Ark finally finished. G dresses as giant cloud for the dedication & adopts cloudwear as his signature formal attire.

LEVITICUS

Overview: Don't eat this. Don't screw that. Don't touch this. Don't *do* that. Thus saith the Lord.

1: Two turtledoves and a partridge in a . . . . Actually, the doves are goners. Don't get attached. A *lot* of animals will die in Leviticus.

2: "Don't even think of giving G an offering with baking soda." I guess I'll have to eat all the chocolate chip cookies myself then.

3: When making a burnt offering, remember: All fat belongs to the Lord. (It seems I won't be getting the chocolate chip cookies after all.)

4: After sinning, roast a scapegoat and let the yummy fat sizzle on up to G. He loves it and will forgive you anything. Good to know.

5: You're unclean if you touch a pig, swear aloud, or sin by accident. Apologize to OCD G, then slaughter a ewe. Rinse. Lather. Repeat.

Five Levitical Laws We Really Hope You're Not Observing

Sure, law in general is a good thing. And some of the laws in Leviticus seem basically harmless to us today—like always including salt in any offering to God, who can't get enough of the stuff despite the high blood pressure the Israelites gave him. But here are some specific Levitical guidelines you might want to let slide.

1. **Cut off any man who has sex with a woman during her period (Lev. 20:18).** By the way, the "cutting off" is only metaphorical here. There are other parts of the Bible where it's not just a metaphor.

2. **Stone anyone who attends Hogwarts (Lev. 20:27).**

3. **Don't allow blind or lame people to be priests.** Also, be sure to avoid dwarves (Lev. 21:18-20). Sorry, Tyrion Lannister.

4. **Kill anyone who curses his parents (Lev. 20:9).**

5. **Stone anyone who blasphemes God (Lev. 24:14).** Since that could include the author of *The Twible* this is a law readers are particularly encouraged to ignore.

6: If you cheat someone, repay the victim AND add 20%. Funny how the Bible's idea of consumer justice is exactly the opposite of Citibank's.

7: Mmm, kidneys. G's favorite! Be sure to include those in your offering. He loves him some steak-and-kidney pie.

8: "Pomp and Circumstance" played at Aaron's 7-day ordination. All those beautiful ephods and tunics get bloodied, Jackson Pollock-style.

9: Family business of Aaron & Sons turns a profit in very first year. No sheep, ox, or goat in Israel is safe from their knives. Chop, chop.

10: Oh no! Two of Aaron's sons lay the altar fire incorrectly, so ever-merciful G burns them up. It's tough to be the preacher's kids.

11: Kosher: Cleft-footed cud chewers and scaly fish. Non-kosher: camels, rabbits, pigs, vultures, and rock badgers. Um, rock badgers?

12: Hey new moms! No sex for 33 days after having a baby boy and 66 days after a girl. Girl germs are much more potent than boy germs.

13: Paging Dr. Aaron: Is it leprosy or just a nice plague? A priest's called to finger a leper. Could the leper be the one missing a finger?

Blind, lame, scabby hunchbacks with crushed
testicles will not be part of the priesthood
recruitment program at this time.

 LEVITICUS **27**

Do Sweat the Small Stuff

"The Bible is full of evidence that God's attention is indeed fixed on the little things. But this is not because God is a Great Cosmic Cop, eager to catch us in minor transgressions, but simply because God loves us—loves us so much that the divine presence is revealed even in the meaningless workings of daily life . . .

   Seen in this light, what strikes many readers as the ludicrous attention to detail in the book of Leviticus, involving God in the minutiae of daily life—all the cooking and cleaning of a people's domestic life—might be revisioned as the very love of God. A God who cares so much as to desire to be present to us in everything we do."

■ Kathleen Norris, *The Quotidian Mysteries*

14: *Leprosy for Dummies.* Seven is the magic number for washing lepers with elaborate rituals. Antibiotics would have also helped.

15: Bodily discharge very bad in both genders. Wash your sheets. Don't even think about having sex. You just thought about it, didn't you?

16: Where's a good scapegoat when we need one? Put our sins on a goat's head and send it to the wild to die already. That'll do it. Or not.

17: No DIY burnt offerings; they only count if supervised by a priest. And don't eat animal blood. Are you listening, Edward Cullen?

18: Incest = bad. Don't go there with your mom, sister, daughter, aunt, or SIL. And don't sacrifice your kids to Molech. Thx.

19: Care for the deaf, blind, poor, and elderly. Avoid tattoos. Don't let cows get it on with sheep. Get rid of Gandalf. And floss daily.

20: More people and animals you can't have sex with. Death penalty for you and the cow. Though why it's the cow's fault we really can't say.

21: Priests are holier than thou. They can't marry widows or divorcees, have a bad hair day, or suffer crushed testicles. Really.

22: Unclean! Priest has cooties if he touches a corpse or a man's semen. He can't eat any ritual offerings until after his shower. Okaaaay.

23: Party all the time, party all the time. For Festival of Booths, make a DIY shack and live in it for a week. Meals not included.

24: Don't curse G or blaspheme, or it's stoning for you. An eye for an eye is the law of the land. Toddlers everywhere approve.

25: Every 7th year, give the land a rest. Every 50th, free some of your slaves & cancel credit card debt. Is this Jubilee or an infomercial?

26: Eagle Scouts get badges for obeying. Be good and you'll get rain and land; disobey and it's a sevenfold plague. Type of plague TBA.

27: Human beings aren't priceless; they cost anywhere from 5 to 50 shekels. Women and girls are worth less than men and boys. Shocker.

NUMBERS

Overview: And now we spend 38 more years in the wilderness (desert, actually). Are we there yet? Look out: heads really roll in this book.

1: Count von Count assists in first-ever census: "One. One tribe of Israel! Two. TWO tribes of Israel! Ah, ah, ah. Next I will count bats."

2: Camp counselor G arranges 603,550 men from 11 tribes; Levites excused from latrine duty *again*. Left. Left. Left, right, left.

3: Some Levites oversee Tabernacle, some the ark, some the sanctuary. They're basically janitors, but prefer to be called sextons.

4: News flash: Ancient Levites were actually Episcopalians. Intense preoccupation with sacred objects, violet cloths, oil, and incense.

5: G banishes lepers from Israel's camp. That's because it's clearly the wish of any loving deity that sick people should die all alone.

6: Nazirites can't eat grapes, drink wine, or cut their hair. Hear that, Samson? "Flow it, show it, as long as God can grow it . . ."

7: On the 12th day of dedication, G's true friends gave to him: 12 oxen, 11 silver platters, 10 shekels, and *lots* of animals to slaughter.

8: How to clean a Levite, age 25-50: Use pure water and go for the full Brazilian wax. No stray hairs, please. Who wants hairy priests?

9: G commands Israel about where and when to camp. Surprise: they actually obey without complaint for two whole chapters!

10: Movin' out, rawhide. Time to blow this Sinai popsicle stand and get on the road. Also: info on the care & feeding of trumpets.

11: Complaining again: "Where's the beef?" Moses is sick of the constant kvetching. G sends quails (yay), followed by a nasty plague (boo).

NUMBERS   **31**

12: More sibling rivalry. Aaron and Miriam wonder why Moses gets the glory. Mir gets a week in a leper tent for this; Aar unscathed. Fair?

13: Isr sends first spies into the Promised Land and find it teeming with huge, scary people. Giants, maybe. This wasn't in the brochure.

14: Isr: "Remind us why you didn't kill us in Egypt?" G: "I sure can't recall. I pronounce a 40-year desert sentence for all you whiners."

15: Or, what happened to Little Timmy when caught gathering wood on the Sabbath. Even Lassie couldn't save him from stoning. Ow.

16: Upstart Levites rise up in mutiny vs. Moses. G buries them mafia-style, then offs another 14,700 Israelites for good measure.

17: Israelites have another panic attack: "We are perishing; we are lost!" Moses adds a pinch of Xanax to their daily manna rations.

18: Firstborn unclean animals can be sold, but firstborn cows and goats are lucky—their blood gets dashed on the altar. They're thrilled!

19: *CSI: Canaan.* All forensic specialists are unclean. Don't touch a corpse, bone, or grave. You will spread Bible cooties.

Worst Careers If You Want to Remain Biblically Clean

The Bible has issues with cleanliness. Well, "issues" is probably the wrong word to use because the laws in Numbers and Deuteronomy despise absolutely anything issuing from the body. But if you want to stay on the right side of the Bible and stay clean, here are some specific jobs to avoid:

• **Gynecologist.** The Old Testament/Hebrew Bible is pretty anxious about blood, women's blood in particular. Menstruation is very, very dangerous, so much so that if you touch or take food from a woman having her period, you're ritually impure. You don't even want to touch her bed, chair, or clothing lest you contract Girl Cooties by osmosis.

• **Undertaker.** If women are impure at least some of the time, the dead are impure all of the time. Ladies, don't you feel better about yourselves, being a step up from corpses?

• **Urologist.** While we're on this medical kick, let's also say that you want to avoid touching men's semen. In fact, you should probably just avoid going to medical school altogether, since you're forever encountering *verboten* bodily fluids there and one of the first things you're expected to do is dissect a dead person.

• **Hog butcher.** In biblical dietary laws, it's not just that you want to avoid eating non-kosher animals like pigs; you don't want to touch them at all. We're sorry, Wilbur. You're a nice pig and all, but we can't hug you.

- **Vampire.** This has become a popular career choice for heroes and heroines of young adult literature, so it's important to note for the record that vampires are inherently impure. Eating any blood, whether from humans or animals, is bad in the eyes of the Bible. Maybe the synthetic stuff they drink on *True Blood* would be okay, but it's best to play it safe and avoid the vampire display altogether when it's time for Career Day at school.
- **Cheeseburger chef.** You can't mix meat and dairy and remain biblically clean, so keep away from Five Guys if you can. (No, I can't seem to stay away from there either. But it's a good idea in theory.)
- **Sacred prostitute.** Surprisingly, the Bible doesn't have a lot of condemnatory things to say about prostitution in general. It's kind of considered an unfortunate fact of life. But if you combine prostitution with the worship of a foreign god, you've crossed over into ritual impurity for sure. So please, no fertility sex acts à la *The Mists of Avalon.*

What to do if you've been exposed to something or someone who is considered a biblical contaminant? Well, the good news is that the Bible is just as obsessed with figuring out how to get rid of cooties as diagnosing how you contracted them in the first place. Your penance might involve a waiting period, some ritual washings, and a few animals sacrificed for good measure.

20: Isr: "There's no water here. Waaaah!" So G brings forth water from a rock. He could've just used his own tears of frustration.

21: Even when Isr asks sweetly, the Amorites won't let them cut through their yard. Isr answers with the sword. Bye-bye, Amorites.

22: Balaam's donkey = the original smartass. The donkey is smarter than Balaam himself, so not much has changed between people and animals.

23: Balaam's hired to curse Israel, but he blesses it 7 times instead. Some people are just determined to focus on the positive.

24: Balaam the "cursing prophet" continues to have only good things to say about Israel. His dastardly Moabite employer's downright pissed.

25: While Balaam was looking on the bright side, Isr was busy screwing up by screwing around with Moabites, so G ices 24,000 whoremongers.

26: To war! You're drafted if you're male, over 20 and breathing. Though with powerful enemies like these you won't be breathing for long.

27: The five daughters of Zelophehad want women to inherit land if there's no male heir, or else one of them will have to marry Mr. Collins.

28: It's Passover! Don't work on first or seventh day. Do sacrifice lambs daily. Don't eat yeasty carbs. And come to Bubbe's for Seder.

29: Most of this chapter is about what G wants you to cook for him during the High Holy Days. Hostess tip: he's totally not a vegetarian.

30: A woman's vow is binding only if it doesn't hassle her hubby. But widows and divorcees are exempt, so lose the guy and call the shots.

31: In Exodus, the Midianites were our friends. But now, G says to kill them all (except the virgins so we can rape them later). Uh, WTF?

32: We're not yet in the Promised Land, but we're already arguing about who will get what once we're there: "Dad, we want THAT pasture!"

33: Aaron dies at age 123, which makes us think that a diet composed solely of manna is maybe not such a bad idea after all.

34: Is it weird for Moses to convey all these land boundaries and allotments, knowing he'll never get to live in the Promised Land himself?

35: If you kill someone by accident, flee to a "refuge city." It's full of people who've committed manslaughter. You'll love it there.

36: Girls, listen up: Yenta will only match you with a guy from your dad's tribe. Gotta keep all that land in the family, see.

DEUTERONOMY

Overview: Moses' Big Speech. Like when you get to Disney but can't enter until after Dad's lecture on how to behave.

1: Apple Maps EPIC FAIL. Journey from A to B should be 11 days, not 40 years. Other 14,589 days like lost weekend.

2: Wow, that Toastmasters class really helped Moses. He's come a long way from being "slow of speech" to a 30-chapter good-bye.

3: Moses recounts old war stories. "We sure trashed them at Bashan! And remember Heshbon? We skunked 'em. Good times."

4: Pep rally continues. "Isn't G the coolest G ever, doing that schtick where he speaks out of fire? And snuffing the Egyptians?"

5: 10 Commandments, Take 2. But now we don't just "remember" the Sabbath; we have to "observe" it. Drat. Farewell, handy loophole.

6: Yo, Israel! The Shema says the Lord is One. Love him with your heart, soul and strength. Tell your kids. Post it on Twitter. Retweet.

7: Rule #1: All indigenous people of Canaan must be destroyed. Rule #2: Don't marry them. (FAQ: If they're destroyed, who's left to marry?)

8: Disneyland will be awesome, with figs, land, and fair housing for all. But don't forget G in the Magic Kingdom, Israel, ya hear?

9: Moses is *still* talking. Like Dad's lectures about how you were ungrateful children and didn't appreciate all his sacrifices. Yada yada.

10: Note to self: always do a backup. Moses uses the Cloud to make a second copy of the stone tablets. Because you just never know.

11: You can win fabulous prizes: choice land, wealth, and sovereignty! But only if you love G and obey. Ah, there's always a catch.

12: Folks, don't make sacrifices just anywhere. G'll show you a special place for that. Oh, and smash other nations' bobblehead gods.

13: Role play this: a friend says a god (not G) spoke to her in a dream. Do you A) run away, B) kill her, or C) join that cult? (It's B.)

Five Deuteronomic Laws We Really Hope You're Not Observing

Just as we saw with Leviticus, there are some biblical laws whose time has, um, passed. Please do not try these things at home.

1. **Kill any family members who don't worship your God (Deut. 13 and 17).** Alas, poor Grandma.

2. **Annihilate any cities that don't worship your God (Deut. 13).** There goes New York.

3. **Rape a woman and then buy her from her father as recompense (Deut. 22:28-29).** Apparently the going bride price for a rape victim is fifty shekels.

4. **Take your wayward kids outside the city gates so the men of the town can stone them to death (Deut. 21:18-21).** We know this is sometimes a tempting option for parents, but please refrain.

5. **Cut off the hand of any woman who, upon seeing her husband in a fight with another man, swoops in and seizes the balls of her husband's opponent (Deut. 25:11-12).** Somehow, this verse never makes it into the canon of passages suitable for cross-stitch. We're not sure why.

14: From "Don't boil a kid in its mom's milk" we extrapolate different pots for meat and dairy. I can't has cheezburger.

15: Yay, you're finally on sabbatical! Aaaah. Too bad you also have to free all your slaves. I mean, graduate students. Ahem.

16: Mo says not to build pillars under any circumstances. Not like he did himself that time. Do what he says, not what he did.

17: Can I get a witness? We could *so* totally stone somebody. We cast the first stones, and then the whole town joins in! Bring a picnic.

18: Don't fry up your kids, cast spells, visit astrologers, or talk to the dead. You're special, Israel, so straighten up and fly right.

19: If you like your neighbor, it's biblically OK to kill him by accident. It's only if you hate him that this is considered murder. Huh.

20: How to do *jihad.* Kill the men and kidnap the women and children. Better yet, just kill everyone. And you thought the Qur'an was violent?

21: If you find a murdered body, kill a cow nearby and have all suspects wash their hands over it. Why don't they do this on *Law & Order*?

22: *What Not to Wear*. Guys, don't wear girls' clothes or mix wool with linen. Also, shirt corners always need tassels. Think 1970s chic.

23: An important penis update: You can't be with holy folk if you're castrated, have crushed testicles, or had a recent wet dream.

24: Misc laws about marriage and divorce, servants, and leprosy. "Will Moses *ever* stop lecturing us? La, la, la; we can't hear you."

25: Henry VIII used these verses on marrying a brother's widow to get Catherine; later used Lev. 20 to divorce her. Convenient to have both.

26: Whenever you pay tithing (once every 3 years), retell the whole wandering Aramean story. Gotta remember your roots, folks.

27: Mo releases an instant bestseller called *12 Curses: A Dozen Reasons Why God Might Want to Smite Your Sorry Ass.* Say amen!

28: Just FYI, Isr, you'll return to an "Egypt" someday. You'll sell your souls to the highest bidder and be slaves. Good luck with that.

29: Mo stops preaching brimstone and gets kinda spiritual, like grandpa right before he croaked. Wait, that means Mo is . . . *oh.*

30: Mo: "G sets before you A) life and prosperity, or B) death and adversity. Oddly, you will choose B, in which case GAME OVER."

It's the Economy, Stupid

Biblical scholar Walter Brueggemann says that the Book of Deuteronomy "classically reimagines life in the world as a neighborly passing for the common good." But this neighbor business is not just about borrowing an occasional cup of sugar in an otherwise capitalist society. Not by a long shot. In *Journey to the Common Good,* Brueggemann provides a list of the "uncommon social ethic" demanded by a Deuteronomic society:

- "Debts owed by the poor are to be canceled after seven years, so that there is no permanent underclass (Deut. 15:1-8): 'Remember that you were a slave in the land of Egypt, and the LORD your God redeemed you'" (v. 15).
- No interest is to be charged on loans to members of the community (Deut. 23:19-20).
- Permanent hospitality is to be extended to runaway slaves (Deut. 23:15-16).
- No collateral is to be required on loans made to poor people (Deut. 24:10-13).
- No withholding of wages that are due to the poor (Deut. 24:14-15).
- No injustice toward a resident alien or an orphan (Deut. 17-18): 'Remember that you were a slave in Egypt and the LORD your God redeemed you' (v. 18)."

Whoa, Nellie! Loans without interest? No permanent underclass? What kind of socialist propaganda is this Bible anyway?

It's unlikely that contemporary American society comes remotely close to this biblical ideal of the just society. However, the people of the Bible didn't exactly walk the walk either, as you'll see when we get to the prophets.

31: Dying Mo names Joshua his successor, but predicts that Isr will fall away no matter who is leading them. These kids today.

32: Mo sings a country ballad about G's achy-breaky heart. G hides face; rips pics from better times. Will Isr give the truck back?

33: Line up to get your deathbed blessing here! All tribes get a flowery word no matter what they've done. Mo's going soft in his last days.

34: Mo's buried in unmarked grave. End of Deuteronomy mimics the start of Genesis in cool ways. Always we begin again. On to Canaan!

JOSHUA

Overview: Toto, we're not in the Torah anymore. And as we enter the Land of Oz, remember to slay anything that moves, OK?

1: G says to be strong and courageous (x 3) in war. People swear to obey Josh just as they did Moses. Cause they did that so well.

2: Israelite spies lack cool gadgets but enlist Bond Girl Rahab to help take Jericho. New literary trope: the whore with a heart of gold.

3: Remember when G drowned the Egyptians in the Red Sea? Now reverses magic so Isr crosses Jordan on dry land. And for his *next* trick . . . .

4: If you're ever at the bottom of the Jordan, tell your kids how G once made dry land there. If you can still breathe, that is.

5: Second-generation Israelites are circumcised before war. The Bible says they spend a while "recovering in camp" afterward. Gee, ya think?

Mount Foreskin

The Bible recounts that Joshua and the tribes of Israel were circumcised before heading into battle, and that the place where all this snipping allegedly occurred was called Gibeath-Haaraloth, roughly translated as, you guessed it, "Hill of Foreskins."

Those Israelites knew how to pick a name everyone would be guaranteed to remember.

The Bible has a thing about foreskins, whether it's here in Joshua or later in 1 Samuel. In that book, a young upstart named David was told that he could marry King Saul's daughter Michal without any kind of bride price if David would only deliver one hundred foreskins of Philistines he'd killed in battle.

Not one to do anything in half measures, David promptly delivered *two* hundred foreskins. Michal gently reminded her new husband that she had also registered at Target and some nice fluffy towels would have been perfectly serviceable instead.

6: Week-long siege of Jericho ends with 7 priests blowing 7 trumpets. City wall flattened; only Rahab spared; Grammy awarded. Awesomesauce.

7: A sinner is duly stoned, then burned, then buried under piles of rubble. It's a "belt and suspenders" approach to discipline.

8: NOW we can take Ai. Josh's military strategy: distract soldiers away so 12,000 men, women, and kids can be hacked to bits. A good day.

9: Foiled! Clever Gibeonites trick Josh into a treaty he has to honor. He can't kill them, but can make them chop wood. So there.

10: G plays War, firing hailstones and stopping the sun during a big battle. He's always first picked for teams, what with the superpowers.

11: The enemy of my enemy is my friend. Foreign kings join forces, having not seen every single action movie where this tactic failed.

12: Nanny nanny, boo boo. List of 31 kings we disgraced and tribes we destroyed. This land is our land, it is not your land . . . .

13: G gave Josh 2 jobs: First, kill Canaanites and grab land. Check! Second, divide land equally among 12 tribes. Hmm, harder than it seems.

14: Loyal Caleb schmoozes old war buddy Josh, who rewards him with the coveted area of Hebron. No, not the one in Kentucky.

15: A strange god lying in an ark distributing land is no basis for a system of government. But lots will be cast. Suck it up.

16: Half-tribe of Ephraim gets a wee inheritance in the south, y'all. Not exactly Texas. More like West Virginia. They're underwhelmed.

17: Josephites (Ephraim + Manasseh) are ticked over their puny real estate. Josh: "Crikey! Knock yourselves out and clear the forest."

18: All tribes stick around until everyone's gotten their land. It's like Mom said: don't leave the table until after everybody's eaten.

19: In case we missed it, the Bible reminds us everyone got their land BY LOT. So get what you get and don't pitch a fit, people.

20: After shedding innocent blood for 19 chapters, now the Bible gets touchy-feely about finding asylum for manslaughter perps. Aaaaw.

21: Disgruntled Levites got nothing in first-draft land pick, so they demand a recount. They're given the best cities. Satisfied now?

A Golden Age. Or Not.

Hold onto your hats, people. In Joshua and Judges, the Bible is about to get even more violent than it was before. Both books are filled with instructions to annihilate any living foreigner, leaving no non-Israelite standing (e.g., 10:28-30).

That means that God in the Bible explicitly orders the massacre of anyone who happened to be living in Canaan and minding their own business before the Israelites showed up.

And how do most of us feel about this today? We love it. We teach Sunday School children about Joshua blowing his trumpet and marching around the walls of Jericho without mentioning the inconvenient little fact that the nice hooker who helped them was the only resident of Jericho still breathing at the end of the day.

Yeah, the Bible is a mess of contradictions. Biblical scholar Gregory Mobley has this to say about it:

> Joshua's era is remembered as a golden age when a prophet like Moses led them (Josh. 1:5; 11:15). With the single exception of one miscreant, Achan in Josh. 7, Joshua and his generation are neither grumblers nor idolaters like their ancestors in the wilderness; they are neither blood feuders nor Baal backsliders like their descendants in the era of Judges.
>
> . . . Biblical authors considered it to be a book with a happy ending (cf. 1 Sam. 12:8; Ps. 105:44-45; Heb. 11:30-31). But the actions described in Joshua are morally reprehensible: genocide, ethnic cleansing, cultural revolutions that seek to eradicate traditional practices, and the seizure of territory from indigenous peoples by colonists who imagine themselves to be righteously entitled.

Is your head exploding yet? Yeah, mine too.

22: Ye gads! 2.5 tribes build an unauthorized altar, then hastily explain that it was only a *memorial*. Yeah, that's the ticket. A memorial.

23: Josh's last pep talk: "Please, please be good. G fought for you, so don't screw it up now. Love G and don't attend those pagan mixers."

24: "Choose this day whom ye will serve." Mad props to the Bible for using the object pronoun "whom" correctly!

JUDGES

Overview: 12 tribal leaders debut reality show: *Judge Judy* meets *COPS*! After more than 200 seasons, king cancels it with all-new lineup.

1: Um, Josh may have inflated that whole "total extinction" thing. The Canaanites were supposed to be dead; many are still here. Oops.

2: Biblical history 101. We cavort with false gods; G uses our enemies to kick our butts; we promise to change; G forgives us. Repeat cycle.

3: Ehud, a lefty judge, slays an obese foreign king before escaping via the rooftop latrine. Yes, really. We're waiting for the movie.

The Crappiest King

Ready for one of the grossest stories in the Old Testament? Well, beating out intense competition in the "disgusting Bible tales" category is an obscure little yarn in Judges 3 about the Israelite judge Ehud killing the Moabite king Eglon. Nowadays it's pretty much only read by scholars, who are intent on parsing its meaning, and junior high boys, who find it scatologically entertaining.

In *The Uncensored Bible: The Bawdy and Naughty Bits of the Good Book*, the authors (biblical scholars who confess to a certain junior high sense of humor themselves) tease out some interesting interpretations of Judges 3. First of all, they say, English translations that offer up vague notions about something "going out" of Eglon upon his assassination are euphemistically avoiding the point: what went "out" of him was his own excrement. The Hebrew word *parshedona*, which only occurs in this story, is hard to translate—which is why any modern translation "probably does not say that Eglon took one final dump when he died." The authors are clear that "the story leaves no doubt that it means that Eglon pooped on himself, which is a normal response to sudden trauma like having a guy stuff a knife into your blubber."

What's more, the authors draw on the work of a fellow scholar to argue that one of the greatest mysteries of biblical history—how did Ehud escape the king's rooftop chambers after the assassination if the only door was locked and guarded?—is easily solved by reference to yet more poop. Yes, the theory is that he exited through the king's latrine. As the book argues, "Ehud's escape through the royal toilet adds the final deliciously repulsive touch to a story already rife with vomit-worthy images."

4: Isr unleashes its secret weapon: Deborah, the OT's very own Eowyn. She's the best judge of all time, though that isn't saying much.

5: Song of Deborah tops charts: "If I had a hammer!" Jael hammers out justice and freedom . . . on Sisera's head. You go, girls.

Jael strikes a decisive blow for Israel.

6: After Deb's halcyon rule comes the first of many flawed judges: Gideon, an A+ whiner. It's only going to get worse from here.

7: Gid may be spiritually lukewarm, but he's *Braveheart* in battle, whuppin' the Midianites. Blow that trumpet, boy.

8: Plot twist! Gid has a hidden agenda: he's not serving G so much as tracking his brothers' killers. Aha. So this is personal.

9: Evil Abimelech kills his 70 brothers with a single stone but is felled by a single unnamed woman wielding a stone. Irony much?

10: Tough love: G's done bailing out the idolatrous Israelites. Lets Ammonites kick ass for 18 years. Isr: "Oops, G! We're so sorry."

11: Jephthah's daughter's fried extra crispy to fulfill his dumb vow. Um, wasn't "no human sacrifice" to be Israel's unique name brand?

12: You say Shibboleth, I say Sibboleth. Sounds like a difference worthy of death to me! Kill our Ephraimite bros. They talk funny.

13: Dr. Angel, OB/GYN, gives prenatal Rx to Samson's mom: Eat kosher, don't drink, and never, ever cut the baby's hair. Got it?

14: Wild X-man Samson kills a lion with his bare hands, then weds a hot Philistine chick. Things don't work out. The Bible's first divorce?

15: Cuckolded Samson skunks 1,000 Philistines armed with only a jawbone. Nevermind what a jawbone is. Just be really impressed.

16: Samson eyes sexy Philistine gal #2; we never learn. Femme fatale Delilah cuts his hair and zaps his strength. Rogaine, anyone?

17: Refrain of "there was no king in Israel" recaps misbehavin' in these last chapters. False gods, shrines, and idols = Bad. No biscuit.

18: Danite spies steal a priest and some ritual stuff from a rival. Kidnapping a priest? That's low, man. Society really does get worse.

19: A Levite's wife is gang raped and chopped up, one piece for each tribe of Israel. Be glad we didn't make this chapter a *Twible* cartoon.

What's a Shibboleth?

Judges 12 has an unusual tale that has contributed a word to our lexicon. After the Gileadites defeated the Ephraimites in battle, the way the victors sorted out the true Gileadites from the fleeing Ephraimite refugees was to perform a little language test.

"Say 'Shibboleth," the Gileadites commanded all who tried to cross the Jordan.

You'd think, in reading this story, that the Ephraimites would be smart enough to pronounce the word exactly the way the Gileadites had just said it: with a "sh" sound at the beginning instead of just the "s" sound they used at home. The Gileadites' enunciating it first was kind of a clue. But the Ephraimites were apparently slow on the uptake as well as inferior in battle, because 42,000 of them fell for the trap and died.

Today, the word "shibboleth" can refer to anything that betrays a person as an outsider to those in the "in" crowd—like, for example, using the word "shibboleth" in conversation when most normal people don't know or care what it means.

Text of Terror

According to the *Women's Bible Commentary*, Judges 19 contains "one of the most brutal, sexually violent, and murderous texts in the entire Hebrew Bible." Biblical scholar Phyllis Trible famously called this a "text of terror" for women. Aren't you super-excited to hear the story?

A Levite and his wife (or concubine; the meaning isn't quite clear) are traveling when a Benjaminite mob bangs on the door of the house where they are staying, demanding that the Levite come out so the crowd can "know" him. This isn't "know" in the form of a friendly welcome-to-the-neighborhood greeting; this is "know" in the we-want-to-know-you-biblically sense. The mob isn't delivering a bundt cake, but preparing to gang rape the Levite.

So the Levite shoves his wife outside and lets the mob gang rape her in his stead.

All. Night. Long. Who says chivalry is dead?

In the morning, when the gangbangers have departed and the coast is clear, the Levite growls at his wife to get up, and when she can't move he heaves her on a donkey for home. But when they arrive, does she receive the medical treatment and lifelong psychiatric therapy she undoubtedly deserves? Hardly. Safely home, he chops her body into twelve pieces and sends one to each tribe of Israel as a protest of his treatment. When the other tribes gather to discuss this outrage, the Levite regales them with his self-promoting version of the story, sparking all-out war against the tribe of Benjamin and the deaths of tens of thousands of people.

20: The Levite asshole gives a selective recap of chapter 19, omitting that he ordered his wife to be raped to save his own skin. Charming.

21: "In those days there was no king in Israel; all the people did what was right in their own eyes." No kidding. Uh, can we get a king now?

RUTH

Overview: Foreign girl wins Israeli edition of *The Bachelor*, thanks to savvy stage mom-in-law. Oh, and BTW? Women rock.

1: Naomi = Best. MIL. Ever. Widowed Ruth sticks to her like glue, changing religions and nationalities just to stay by her side. LYLAS, Ma.

2: Jane Austen plot in ancient setting! Destitute Ruth goes a-gleanin' and meets eligible bachelor Boaz Darcy, who saves her family.

3: Ruth lies down at Boaz's "feet" (wink, nudge). Any nun will tell you that girls can get pregnant that way. Do I hear wedding bells?

4: Ruth and Boaz marry and have David's grandpa. If the king comes from a foreign great-grandma, maybe God loves EVERYONE, not just Israel?

Did She Or Didn't She?

Many people have invested significant effort into proving whether Ruth did or did not seduce Boaz on the threshing room floor. What's really going on in chapter 3?

For the record, *The Twible* thinks that the internal evidence for seduction is all over the biblical text. Naomi tells Ruth to dress in her finest, anoint herself with oil, and go find her kinsman Boaz on the threshing room floor, a site as notorious for nighttime thrashing as daytime threshing. Ruth does this, waiting until Boaz is asleep before she uncovers his "feet"—a well-known biblical euphemism for another part of the male anatomy entirely—and lies down next to him. The next day, they are engaged.

But maybe we're all asking the wrong questions. In The *Story of Ruth*, spirituality writer Joan Chittister says that these are in fact "sad, pathetic questions, not because they titillate or smirk or smack of presumption but because they so obscure what is really at issue here." This episode, Chittister says, is not about sex but about "what it means to take your life into your own hands." Ruth and Naomi refuse to simply be victims after all the tragedies life has doled out to them; they will not wait around to be rescued. "They change things in a society that says that women are not its changers and that nothing can be changed," writes Chittister.

For that they are heroes.

1 SAMUEL

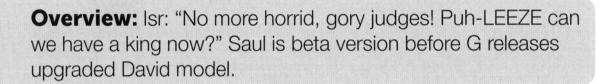

Overview: Isr: "No more horrid, gory judges! Puh-LEEZE can we have a king now?" Saul is beta version before G releases upgraded David model.

1: Is Hannah A) drunk in the temple, or B) praying like hell for a son? (It's B. Some folks just look wasted when they pray. It's a thing.)

2: Hannah croons a rock ballad to G: "Finally, a son! My Samuel is here! G answered me!" She can't fight this feelin' any longer.

3: In boyhood, Sam hears a voice calling him, but it's G. The DSM says this is perhaps not the best psychiatric model for kids today.

4: Israel routed by Philistines! Ark captured. (That's like when someone steals your college mascot, except that folks also tend to die.)

5: Phils find ark a mixed blessing when it chops off their god's head and hands. Ark now a hot potato: Get it outta town!

6: Phils hire Martha Stewart for advice on a gift to send back with the ark so G won't roast them. Gold's always appropriate.

7: Grown-up Sam gets Isr back on track; becomes circuit judge. Repentant Isr finally able to kick Phils' butts. G's baa-ack!

8: Sam warns: "A king will take your land and kids, start wars, and enslave you. Danger ahead!" Isr: "Sounds cool. Where do we sign?"

9: Lost donkeys are a McGuffin to set up Saul as the kind of guy who'd seek lost donkeys. Sam is his talent scout: "Stick with me, kid."

10: Silent sons never change. Returning home from Sam's, all Saul says is, "The donkeys are OK." Not, "Hi Ma, and BTW I'm king now."

11: Saul makes his bid for kingship the old-fashioned way: hacking an enemy to shreds. Ah, the good old days. Coronation!

12: You know how Obi-Wan has to vanish after Luke's a Jedi? With Saul as king, Sam exits stage left, lecturing all the way.

13: First occurrence of "land of Israel." We're a real country now, people. No more wee clans and land plots!

14: Saul's son Jonathan doesn't get the memo about not eating honey. Mean Saul curses him. The people stand up for Jon. Power to the people!

15: G has second thoughts about Saul as king. Obi-Sam returns as guest star to tell Saul he's on his own because G's rejected him. Uh oh.

16: *Star Search.* G wants Sam to anoint one of Jesse's eight sons as king. David's the runt of the litter, but G picks him anyway. Some pig!

17: Dave fells giant Goliath with a slingshot. Amazing! Inducted with Rocky, the Karate Kid, and Susan Boyle into Underdog Hall of Fame.

18: Dave is Saul's top guy and a chick magnet. But Saul's jealous and starts trying to kill him. It's always something.

19: Michal defies Saul, her own dad, to save the usurper Dave from certain death. In this family, blood < water.

20: Bible's finest bromance. Dave + Jon = BFFs. Jon disobeys Saul to protect Dave. Bitter tears and pinky promises at parting. Sniff.

21: Celeb sighting! Dave flees Saul, but the locals recognize him and call TMZ. Dave pretends to be crazy, which isn't a huge stretch.

22: Dave's lost weekend. Hides out in a cave writing songs, then gathers a ragtag band with 400 rejects. You say you want a revolution?

23: Wicked Saul plays hide-and-seek with Dave. Saul: "Where are you, runt? Mwahaha." Dave: "What is your deal, king? What'd I do?"

24: Dave has a golden opportunity to kill while Saul is on the throne. Um, the OTHER throne. However, Dave's too noble. For the moment.

25: Dave charms the socks off Nabal's wife Abigail, who risks all to help him. When her hubby dies, Dave makes her wife #2. So it begins.

26: Dave has a second chance to kill Saul; again resists. Saul again swears not to hunt him: "Bless you, Dave!" Yeah, right.

27: Dave takes junior year abroad with Phils and goes native. Where better to escape Saul? But is Dave a sleeper agent . . . or a traitor?

28: Saul, quaking in his sandals about the Philistine threat, conjures an irritated Sam from the dead. Sam says Saul's a dead king walking.

29: Phils distrust Dave despite his apparent record as a traitor to Isr. They send him back home. It seems they recall Goliath.

30: Israelite wives taken captive. Rescue mission! Dave saves every damsel in distress. MORPG videogame version currently in development.

31: Saul and 3 sons die in battle, including Jon. Noooo. Dave's grief will be a force to reckon with when he hears. Cue theme from *Love Story.*

2 SAMUEL

Overview: Like 1 Sam but with focus on Dave, who Vaders up fast as king. Sex, blood, and murder make for strong box office $$.

1: Dave's so sad about Saul and Jon that he shoots the messenger—literally. Releases new #1 song: "Oh, how the mighty have fallen!"

2: Dave's now king of Judah, the southern region, but Saul's last son is king up north . . . for now. Time to destroy the demilitarized zone.

3: Li'l Abner switches sides to support Dave but Joab slays him anyway for good cartoon fun. Now Dave's the saddest man in Dogpatch.

4: Dave's overzealous chiefs kill Saul's last son and bring Dave his head. It doesn't end well for the chiefs. New job opening?

The United Monarchy

Before we get much further into the Old Testament/Hebrew Bible, we need to know a little bit about the United Monarchy.

Basically, this was one brief shining moment of unity between the northern and southern regions of Bibleland. That period under the kingships of Saul, David, and Solomon lasted for roughly a century, from about 1030 to 930 BCE. Before that, the twelve tribes of Israel (and the other unfortunate folks who were already living in the area) had a pretty loose and bloody system of government under the reign of the judges. Not a particularly fun time.

Kingship consolidated wealth, power, and land in the hands of a single person. As we see in 1 and 2 Samuel, though, absolute power tends to corrupt absolutely. Even though each of those three kings was chosen by God, each of them missed the mark in some way. Saul was a jealous sort, trying to kill the upstart David and ignoring God's commandment about the spoils of war (1 Sam. 15). David, the young underdog of 1 Samuel, changed a great deal over time, going from an innocent young shepherd to the kind of king who had a neighbor killed just so he could sleep with the guy's wife. And David's son Solomon was even more complicated, obeying God's commandments in some things, like building a temple, while living high and subjugating people through slavery. (Those slabs of rock that built the temple? That was slave labor, baby.)

What's interesting about 1 and 2 Samuel is that the books preserve these kings in all their complexity, allowing us to see the good, the bad, and the ugly. Even though the kings of the United Monarchy weren't perfect, they were a darn sight better than many of the kings that came after Israel split in half, a period we'll get to soon.

5: Israel united, N and S together! Dave's king! Take lots of pics now and smile for the camera, because these happy days won't last.

6: Dave's a contestant on *So You Think You Can Dance Before the Ark of the Lord?* His wife Michal's a judge. She's *not* happy with his act.

7: G hankers for a cedar home in Jerusalem, ranked as the #1 city for deities to retire. Good son Dave promises to visit often.

8: Dave crushes Amalekites, Philistines, Syrians, and others. Awesome spoils in slaves, gold, brass, and chariots. Hail to the King!

9: Dave seeks out Jon's lame son, all grown up now, for Jon's sake. Dave still mourns his old BFF. Shucks, where's my hanky?

10: Ammonites mock Dave's envoys by shaving their beards and exposing their butt cheeks. Humph! "Go away or we will taunt you a second time."

11: Dave knocks up bathing beauty Bathsheba, then kills off her virtuous hubby in army "accident." There goes the monarchy.

12: Prophet Nathan raps to Dave: "Remember the gangsta who plucked a berry, then iced her guy? You da man! But not in a good way."

13: Dave's son Amnon rapes his half-sister Tamar. Blech. The whole family's livid, but it's Absalom who gets revenge. Take that, Amnon. Die!

14: Dave won't touch a hair on Abs's head if he'll only come home. This is saying something because Abs is known to be very hairy.

15: Chickens come home to roost. Abs conspires vs. Dave; prints "Vote for Absalom" signs and rises in polls. 90% approval rating.

16: In chapter 12, Nathan warned Dave that evil would arise in his own house. Now in 16: Hello, Evil Son. Please stop screwing your stepmoms.

17: Double agent Hushai nixes simple a assassination plot in favor of a huge, stupid, unwinnable war. Military leaders say, "Sure!"

18: Shakespearean tragedy. Loyalist Gen. Joab defeats rebels, staking his cousin Abs through the heart. What happened to "deal gently"?

19: Oh Absalom, Absalom! Joab has to tell Dave to snap out of his grief and make a public appearance. Wave, now. Elbow, elbow, wrist, wrist.

20: Just when we thought the Empire had crushed the Rebellion, some tribes get uppity. Sequels are never quite as good, are they?

EXIT POLLS

And You Thought Your Family Was Messed Up?: A Fairy Tale

Once upon a very dysfunctional time, a king had way too many sons. By custom, the oldest was probably supposed to inherit the throne, but a much younger son did instead. How did this happen?

First, the oldest son raped one of his half-sisters. Son #3 was as grossed out about this as you probably are in reading the story, so he handily arranged the death of Son #1. Since Son #2 was either dead or not interested in ruling (the fairy tale is unclear on this point), Son #3 started clamoring to be the heir after Son #1 was out of the picture. Son #3 staked his claim by having sex with his father's wives and concubines and by rebelling in general. (In his mind, sleeping with one's stepmothers was apparently fine, but sleeping with one's half-sister was punishable by death.)

Son #3 got killed rather gruesomely in battle against the king's troops during the revolt he started, leaving only Sons #4 and #5 to contend for the throne. But the mother of Son #5 begged the king to have her son anointed as the heir apparent, which the now-feeble king did before he died. Displaced Son #4 skipped town for a while, then tried to stage a coup, after which Son #5, now king, had Son #4 summarily executed.

And they all lived happily ever after on Showtime. The ones who managed to stay alive, anyway.

21: The appendix of 2 Sam has stuff we wanted to include but couldn't fit, like about Dave killing Saul's 7 sons. (Huh? 2 Sam Version 2.0.)

22: Dave feels a song coming on. "Yay God, who rescued me from harm and made me king; Yay God, who lets me get away with anything!"

23: We're *still* not finished yet. Appendix further proves that history's written by the winners. And their scribes.

24: G's mad (where'd that come from?) and he's not gonna take it anymore. It's Yahweh or the highway, baby.

1 KINGS

Overview: Solomon holds monarchy together, but it's splitsville after his death. Northern and southern kingdoms with lots of wicked kings.

1: Son #3 plots vs. Dave. (Why'd he want so many sons, anyway?) But #5 son Sol wins king sweepstakes. We predict big things.

2: Dying Dave advises Sol to follow Torah, but also to murder his rivals now while he still can. So spiritual, yet so practical.

3: Sol marries Pharaoh's girl and thinks he should Walk Like an Egyptian. New temple seen on *Lifestyles of the Rich & Infamous*.

4: *The Godfather.* Sol's the man you can't refuse *and* the wise author of 300+ proverbs about simplicity and family values. Go figure.

5: "Forced labor" is nice way of saying "Slaves R Us." Sol gives Phar a run for his money in the race for who's more cruel. It's a toss-up.

Solomon and his happy family

6: Holy, holy, holy? G's private spa inside the temple is decked out with gold everywhere and a Levite massage therapist trained in Sweden.

7: Solomon deforests Lebanon to build the fanciest palace around, then a temple with pillars so big they even have individual names. Showoff.

8: The temple dedication's a bloodbath: 22,000 oxen and 120,000 sheep. Oh man, what'll be left to eat when Sol's prayer is finally over?

9: Congrats, peon. You're now drafted into Sol's army. Or you may be one of the slaves who finishes the temple. Lucky you, huh?

10: Sol's a cutthroat arms dealer, supplying the Hittites. The Queen of Sheba visits him for a regional gun convention.

11: *Sister Wives* has nothing on Sol, who keeps 700 princesses and 300 concubines. Remind him whose night it is, again?

12: Uh oh, the kingdom's divided. Sol's son Rehoboam's king of South and Jeroboam's king of North. Both break out BIG bottles of champagne.

13: Jero sets up DIY altar in North. His people love the golden calf, but G's not so crazy about it. Puts Jero on the naughty list.

14: OK, that's it. After 22 yrs, G's done with Jero and all his kin. (Doggies, here's supper!) Reho's not much better in the South.

North and South

After Solomon's death, those nice cozy days of the United Monarchy came to an end. The southern and northern regions hadn't always been best buds anyway, and those fissures widened into gaping chasms when it came time to crown Solomon's successor.

For a while it looked like Solomon's son Rehoboam would be king over a full and united empire, just like his father. But those irksome ten tribes up in the north had other ideas. They weren't thrilled about the heavy taxes Solomon had levied against them to build a temple way down south in Jerusalem, and they feared that Rehoboam's kingship would just mean more of the same. They were right; Rehoboam's taxes were even worse than Dear Old Dad's. The northern tribes were having none of it. So around 930 BCE they set up their own King of the North, just like in the novel *Game of Thrones*, which they had all read cover to cover.

The northern kingdom was called Israel (which is really confusing because that's also the name the Bible often uses to refer to the whole united country) and the southern kingdom was named Judah. Judah was smaller, but it controlled a lot of resources, including the capital city of Jerusalem with its small but lavish temple.

What happens in the rest of 1 and 2 Kings is like an accelerating tragedy. You know it's going to be a train wreck, and that each ruler of both the northern and southern kingdoms will be even worse than the last, but you just can't tear yourself away. (Idolatry? Check. Child sacrifice? Check.) And while there are brief moments of unity, like at the end of 1 Kings when the North and South temporarily join forces against a common enemy, the general arc of the story is one of dissolution and despair. And that's *before* the exile. So brace yourself.

15: Good king, bad king. They never seem to last long these days. Old Dave and Sol are actually looking pretty appealing about now.

16: King Ahab of Israel marries *shiksa* Jezebel and starts worshipping Baal. Ahab's so wicked the other kings look like choirboys.

17: Recap: The kingdom's split in two; Baal worship is all the rage; G's forgotten. Or is he? Enter Elijah, our hero prophet, stage left.

18: Theology throwdown; Elij dares 850 pagan prophets to duel. Elij: "Ha! Is that all you've got? LMAO @ your girly-man gods."

19: Elij crashes from theological high; now in deep funk sans Celexa. Wants to die, but G won't hear of it. Bakes him a cake instead.

20: Ahab offers *some* of his gold, wives, and kids to invaders, but not *all* like they demand. (He still likes that one wife.) To war!

21: Queen Jezebel uses eminent domain to seize a vineyard, then has the owner stoned. Don't worry, though. She'll soon be Pupperoni.

22: Great Jehoshaphat! Kings of North and South join forces to fight Syrians. Book ends on happy note of unity and peace, which won't last.

Prophet Death Match

One of the most famous stories in 1 Kings relates the prophet Elijah's conflict with the 850 prophets of the foreign deities Baal and Asherah. The context for this scene is that it hasn't rained in the northern kingdom of Israel for more than three years—a drought that Elijah himself helped put into place. Disgusted by the antics of Israel's kings, Elijah had reached his nadir when a leader ritually sacrificed his own sons during the refortification of Jericho (1 Kings 16:34–17:1). Since the God of Israel unequivocally drew the line at human sacrifice, Elijah declared that there wouldn't be so much as a drop of rain or dew until the prophet gave the all-clear.

So when our story begins, Israel's people are desperate and starving, having been several years without rain. It is in this situation that Elijah throws down a gauntlet: he's going to vie single-handedly against 850 of the prophets of the king's foreign gods. Who among them can successfully conjure fire to burn an animal sacrifice?

The story is pretty comical. The foreign prophets go first, preparing an ox for sacrifice and desperately praying to Baal all morning long to do something, anything, to get the fire going. Loads of people gather to watch the spectacle. (They would have brought a picnic and made a day of it if they'd had any food whatsoever.)

Elijah ruthlessly taunts the foreign prophets: Maybe Baal is off practicing Zen meditation somewhere? Maybe he's sunning himself on a Mediterranean cruise? Or maybe he's getting some beauty sleep and has forgotten to set the alarm? Wherever Baal is, he's certainly not answering.

Then it's Elijah's turn. He takes his time about it too; the Bible gives us numerous details about how he builds an altar out of twelve stones, lays the firewood just so, and carefully butchers an ox in preparation. Then twelve buckets of water are thrown onto the ox and the firewood, just to make it even more miraculous when the whole sacrifice blazes up the moment Elijah prays to the God of Israel. Even the water itself is aflame, a nifty trick.

The prophets of Baal start to flee in fear, but Elijah's having none of that. He orders the people to seize and massacre all 850 false prophets, adding to the Bible's already impressive body count.

And then, at last, there is rain.

2 KINGS

Overview: Now entering the Royal Tragedy Zone. Most kings are lousy, which is why this story won't end well. Exile . . . ? Sob.

1: King has nasty fall and goes to Baal Hospital for consult. Out of network! G's own Dr. Elijah puts king on bed rest . . . FOREVER.

2: Elij goes out in style in BMW Fire Chariot to heaven. Elisha gets Elij's spirit times 2. Look out, world! Elisha = Miracle Max.

3: Routed Moabite king craves power of Ab's near-sacrifice of Isaac. No ram shows up this time, though. "Whoopsies! Sorry, son."

4: Elisha multiplies oil, purifies food, and feeds the poor. Can we hire him as a consultant on the Middle East and the environment?

5: Elisha has no Magic Leprosy Wand? Naaman's ticked. But after washing 7 times, he's a convert. Bonus: he gets to keep his nose.

6: Elisha's YouTube videos go viral! But when famine comes and folks eat their own kids, he gets blamed. You just can't win.

10 Biblical Names That Shouldn't Be Used Again Anytime Soon

Biblical names are making a comeback nowadays. According to the Social Security Administration, among the most popular boys' names of 2012 were Jacob, Noah, Ethan, and Michael; and you can't seem to throw a stone at a sinner without hitting an Abigail or a Hannah. My own daughter's name is Jerusha (2 Kings 15), which is odd but not bizarre enough for her to hate me when she's all grown up. Here's hoping, anyway.

But some biblical names aren't seen much, and for good reason. Here are ten that should stay good and buried.

Girls

Lo-Ruhamah (Hos. 1)
> This name means "not loved" or "not pitied." Please tell me you'll give your daughter a better welcome in life than this.

Hepzibah (2 Kings 21)
> Yeah, I know there is a Harry Potter character with this name, as well as a Marvel Comics character. And I know that the word has connotations of "delight" in Hebrew. But the name itself sounds like a hiccup.

Oholibamah (Gen. 36)
> This name spawns holiness jokes *and* Obama jokes. The poor girl.

Rahab (Josh. 2)
> Do you really want to name your daughter after a prostitute?

Gomer (Hos. 1)
> Yeah, another prostitute. Plus there would be all those endless Gomer Pyle jokes.

Boys

Ham (Gen. 9)
> This name basically guarantees your son a future in mediocre comedy. It's all down to you, Mom and Dad.

Mash (Gen. 10)
> Seriously? *Mash*? If a name ever shouted, "Beat me up on the playground!" this is it.

Shammuah (2 Sam. 5)
> The last I heard, this was a whale's name. Let's just not go there.

Dodo (Judges 10, 2 Sam. 23, and 1 Chron. 27)
> According to the *Holman Bible Dictionary*, this name actually has a beautiful meaning: "his beloved." But I guarantee that if you give your son this name, he won't be feeling the love.

Jehoshaphat (2 Chron. 20)
> "Great _____ !" Enough said.

7: Turnaround! Arameans are sent packing; Isr has plenty to eat; Elisha is back in good graces. Wait, is that the other shoe dropping?

8: Elisha, consulted about an ill king, says in a stage whisper, "He's gonna die, but why tell him? BTW, my fee's 40 camel-loads of stuff."

9: Alpo Corporation tests new "Jezebel" flavor; wins canine pre-approval in focus group. Lick it up, dogs. Wait, you missed a spot.

10: Slaughter of Baal followers. Take that, Baal! You're the one who liked human sacrifice. Your temple's our new port-a-potty.

11: Queen Athaliah tries to wipe out the whole Davidic line, but Prince Joash hides in temple for 6 years playing video games. Saved!

12: Joash grows up to be a good king, but G's temple has seen better days. Joash says it's time for *Real Estate Intervention.*

13: Elisha dies, but he's *still* doing miracles: a dead guy who just touches Elisha's bones comes back to life. Overachiever.

14: Dear Judah: Now that you and Israel face annihilation from Assyria, this is the perfect time to kill EACH OTHER! Have at it.

15: (We interrupt *The Twible* to announce a sighting of Jerusha, a don't-blink-or-you'll-miss-her queen. That's my girl.)

16: Judah sinks ever lower as its king brown-noses Assyria by redesigning the temple altar to fit Assyria's god. Now they're in for it.

17: Crap. It's 722 BCE; idolatrous Israel's conquered by Assyria. Your time's coming, Judah, so wipe that smirk off your face.

Now, Where Did I Put That Deuteronomy Scroll?

You never know what you're going to discover when you declutter: old hockey sticks? Stuffed bears? Lawn sculptures? So when young king Josiah gave orders around 621 BCE that the dirty, disused Jerusalem temple should be cleaned out and spruced up, he probably never expected that it would be the beginning of a whole new phase in Israel's nationhood. (See? Organizing really can change your life.)

When Josiah's high priest Hilkiah was clearing out the treasure room, he found a special scroll. We're not precisely certain what was in it—either a copy of the first five books of the Bible or just the Book of Deuteronomy by itself. Hilkiah brought the scroll to Josiah: "Hey, whaddya think we ought to do with this?"

Instead of selling it on eBay, Josiah decided to read it for himself, and was so shaken by what he learned that he tore his clothes—a sign of terrible grief. He was shocked to learn of these laws that he knew his people had not been obeying, and afraid that God would punish Judah if they didn't fall in line ASAP.

Josiah read the scroll out loud to the people and then made them start living God's statutes. He outlawed the worship of foreign gods and banished pagan cults from the Jerusalem temple, where several had taken up a very cozy residence. He had the people start keeping the Passover festival again, and he executed loads of foreign priests.

Josiah was praised for all these reforms, but Judah's foxhole conversion wasn't quite enough to appease God. The prophetess Huldah told Josiah that because God approved of all the changes he had made, Josiah would die before the coming destruction of Judah. He personally was safe. However, said destruction was still going to go down despite the nation's newfound religiosity.

Josiah reigned until 609 BCE, and the few Judean kings who succeeded him (including some of his own sons) didn't do as fine a job in holding the monarchy or the nation's religion together. With enemies like Egypt and Babylon nipping at their heels, they had short and tumultuous reigns. The last king was Zedekiah (which is easy to remember when you recall that Zed is the last letter of the alphabet), who reigned until the Babylonian exile. The Babylonian invaders let Zedekiah keep his eyesight just so he could watch his sons be murdered. Then they put his eyes out, took him captive, and made him live the rest of his days in chains.

18: 701 BCE. Judah holds out vs. Assyrians; finally gets a righteous king. Cause with a name like Hezekiah, he HAS to be good.

19: Miracle rescue! G saves Judah from Assyrians and Judah can do no wrong. G'll always bail us out . . . right? Uh, hello?

20: Flashback 15 years earlier when G told a sick Hez that Judah would be safe for 15 years. Which means . . . fasten your seat belts.

21: Manasseh = Worst. King. Ever. Which is especially bad since he reigned for 55 *years*. Child sacrifice and the whole enchilada.

22: 621 BCE. Reformer King Josiah: "Now, where did I put that Deuteronomy scroll? This temple is so cluttered, I can't find . . . Aha!"

23: Pious Josiah uses Book of Deuteronomy to remake Judah according to G's wishes. But prophetess Huldah says it's too late. Party pooper.

24: 587 BCE, a date that shall live in infamy. Babylonians sack Jerusalem and raze its temple. Where's the comedy in exile?

1 CHRONICLES

Overview: 1 and 2 Chronicles offer a remedial OT overview in case you were sleeping. Pomo retread of the same stories from other POVs.

1: Chronicler binges on genealogy for 9 freakin' chapters. Begat, begat. He must be retired with lots of time on his hands for family trees.

2: The tribe of Judah gets Tamargate (Gen. 38) erased from its story. History always looks nobler in hindsight, eh?

3: Main point of genealogy detour: David rocks! We ♥ you, David! You were the best king ever. Fanzines available at 1-900-KINGDAV.

4: Obscure Judahite named Jabez makes the most of a walk-on part, selling 9 million copies of schmaltzy prayer. "Expand my borders" indeed.

5: Also-ran tribes of Simeon, Reuben, etc. get their due, but where are the Zebulonites and Danites? Excised from the record. Hmm.

6: Levite genealogy repeats the same stock names, because Zadok is such a cool name you're gonna want 6 or more in each generation.

7: Ephraimites get wiped out in cattle raid until Ephraim starts again with family #2. Saves the tribe, but names firstborn "disaster." Ow.

8: Smallest tribe of Benjamin gets longest shout-out; how is THAT fair? "Mom, I'm bigger than he is! Why's he your favorite?"

9: Here endeth the begats. Finally! Now we turn to Saul, who's not a real king here. More of a warm-up act for Dave, the hero of Chronicles.

10: A prosaic view is that Saul offs himself—the only suicide in the OT. Chronicler's view: he dies of unfaithfulness, like spiritual H1N1.

11: In this utopian history, Jerusalem falls without a struggle, all 12 tribes instantly unite behind King Dave, and unicorns are real.

12: 339,600 troops gather with one heart to crown Dave king. Celebrate good times! All Israel goes on a 3-day bender. Details censored.

13: It's all fun and games until Uzzah touches the ark. (Bad idea. Die.) Dave checks the ark into a hotel as he ponders his next move.

14: We interrupt this story of Dave's failure to bring the ark to Jerusalem with 3 success stories. Because after all, Dave is awesome.

15: Levites only in the ark processional, please. All other arklifters will be roasted. Thank you for your cooperation.

16: The ark's in Jerusalem, baby! But PG version of the story omits Dave's full frontal nudity. No ark pole-dancing here, no sir.

17: G wants a dream house in Jerusalem, and his wish list includes cedar shingles and a chapel. But he fires Dave as general contractor.

18: Dave may not be G's first choice as a homebuilder, but he cleans up on the battlefield. Sayonara, Moabites and Edomites.

19: Dave sends mourners to an Ammonite royal funeral, but they attack Isr instead. Sheesh. Some people are just so testy.

20: Where Bathsheba tale SHOULD go. (SOS, huge lacuna!) The Chronicler wants to show the best of Dave, not the warts. But warts are fun.

21: Are you ready for Dave's greatest sin? Wait for it . . . the CENSUS. Yes, unauthorized censuses can result in plague. Oh.

22: Usually Chronicles ♥s Dave, but here's a tale not in 2 Sam: Dave's temple bid is nixed because of his violence. Coen Bros also flat out.

23: Can you please pass the whitewash? We need to Photoshop out that pesky Absalom coup story. Thx. (P.S. Solomon rules.)

24: On priests and Levites. Aaronic priests do the animal sacrifices and the Levites clean up afterward. Someone has to do the housework.

25: Wanted: temple musicians. Must play lute, harp, and cymbal. Prophetic ability and experience preferred. Family heritage a plus.

26: Wanted: temple gatekeepers, also known as bouncers. Don't bother applying, though. We'll cast lots and call you soon.

27: Dave leaves Solomon with a stable military, swelling coffers, and a fully stocked minibar. NOW Sol can build the temple.

28: Dave says good-bye. Sniff. Advises new king Sol that when playing hide-and-seek with G, it's good to let G find you.

29: OK, Israel. Time to pony up for the temple pledge drive. Make that call! Or you can donate online at stonebystone. com.

What's Missing from the David Story?

Every king needs a royal biographer to make him look good. History is written by the winners, after all. This becomes clear when we compare the David narratives from 1 Chronicles with the same stories in 1 and 2 Samuel. In keeping with the Chronicler's desire to present David and his dynasty in the best possible light, there's a lot missing.

- **Saul is dispatched in a mere fourteen verses (1 Chron. 10:1–14).** Whereas much of 1 Samuel details Saul's call, rise to kingship, military conquests, and eventual fall from grace, 1 Chronicles couldn't care less about him. Saul is merely the five-minute opening act before the real star appears.
- **Saul's death is decidedly ignominious.** Whereas in Samuel he's killed in battle, the Chronicler has King Saul committing suicide—the only suicide in the entire Old Testament.
- **David does not dance naked before the Ark.** Granted, as the story is related in 1 Samuel, it's not obvious that David was completely naked, but however he was attired was enough to shock his wife. In the Chronicler's account, by contrast, there's no dancing of any kind, exotic or otherwise. David does make one mistake in his eagerness to obtain the Ark, hastily grabbing it himself instead of letting the Levites do their job. But he only makes this error because of his great religious devotion, and by the way, did the Chronicler mention that David is 110 percent awesome?
- **David never seduces Bathsheba or orders the murder of her husband.** Perhaps the most glaring omission from the Chronicler's account is the total whitewash of David's greatest sins. Some commentaries have excused this by saying that the story of David's personal life is unrelated to the larger narrative of Israel and Judah, and was therefore left out because it wasn't important to national history. Seriously? Considering that the next king of Israel is a guy named Solomon—the direct fruit of the adulterous relationship between David and Bathsheba—it's hardly irrelevant. And since when did God make a distinction between public and private lives for any other king of Israel or Judah?

- **David clearly passes the throne on to Solomon, and there's no bloody war of succession.** In fact, the rebellious Absalom is barely mentioned in 1 Chronicles. David declares before God and around 38,000 priests that he has appointed Solomon to be the next king, and the people couldn't be more pleased. End of story. Move along. Nothing to see here, folks.

In sum, the moral of Chronicles is that the sun shines out of David's butt. Not that we've ever seen his butt, because he never, ever danced naked before God and everybody.

2 CHRONICLES

Overview: Like 2 Kings, but with northern kings and history removed. This is SOUTHERN history, y'all.

1: G grants Sol a wish. Instead of wishing for more wishes, he asks for wisdom. What's wise about that? But G approves.

2: Sol needs cheap (read: "free") labor for the temple, so he hires (read: "enslaves") 153,600 foreigners to do it. Holy, holy.

3: Gild that lily, Sol! Temple walls, etc. covered in gold paneling. Even the nails are gilded. Silver was *so* last year.

4: Temple Decor 101: Huge basin of water resting on 12 oxen; bronze altar for animal sacrifice; golden lamps. It's Vegas, baby.

5: Musicians do such a fine job at the temple dedication that G comes as a cloud. Ladies and gentlemen, G has entered the building.

Inside Solomon's Temple

The opening chapters of 2 Chronicles are filled with descriptions of the wonders of God's much-anticipated temple in Jerusalem, and with a record of its looooong ceremonial dedication. The temple housed the Ark of the Covenant, and was the site where Sanctioned and Approved Official Animal Sacrifices could take place. Other people in the Bible tried to make sacrifices and offerings closer to home—it was a long way to the temple after all, particularly for those stubbornly independent types up north—but the Bible takes a dim view of such decentralization. The Jerusalem temple was the place to be, worship-wise, and it was decked out accordingly.

Having said that, Solomon's temple was surprisingly small. The Bible gives its dimensions by cubit, which Old Testament scholar John Goldingay says would be about half a yard. In his popular translation *The Message*, Eugene Peterson portrays the temple's overall dimensions in feet, a measurement North American readers are more likely to understand; Peterson says the building was about ninety feet long and thirty feet wide. If that figure is accurate, that's just 2,700 square feet total, which is not much larger than the average new-construction American home. By contrast, a Walmart Supercenter clocks in at an average of 187,000 square feet, and some box stores have exceeded a quarter of a million square feet of real estate.

In other words, a hundred Jerusalem temples could fit into a single one of those über-super-mega box stores and shop for their candles, tank tops, candy bars, and any other items that self-respecting temples might need.

But the temple building was never intended to accommodate a crowd of people; it wasn't a place where a whole congregation met for worship. If folks wanted to gather, there was a large courtyard just outside the temple for that purpose. The temple was built as a house for God to dwell in, and the specific studio apartment where God lived—the "Holy of Holies" at the back of the temple—was only entered by a single person on a single day each year.

6: Sol: Oh G, hear each prayer that will go up from this temple. Protect us from plague, famine, and very hungry caterpillars.

7: Animals, now that those long prayers are over, it's time for you to die on the altar. Sorry about that. It's a God thing.

8: Oh, yeah! We forgot that Sol is a king in addition to the temple go-to guy. Quick bullet points of other CV items.

9: Queen of Sheba (now Yemen?) showers Sol with gold and jewels because he's the rock star of the ancient world. We're not worthy.

10: Sol dies after ruling 40 years and sleeps with his ancestors. No, not THAT kind of sleeping, you necro. Hello, divided kingdom.

11: Northern king sets up illegitimate shrines. Very bad! After this, Chronicler ignores the 10 Lost Tribes. 4 8 15 16 23 42.

12: "Other deeds of Rehoboam are recorded in books by the prophet Shemaiah and the seer Iddo." And these books are where, exactly?

13: Judah's king lectures Isr on battlefield: "You deserted G, the temple, and the valid priesthood, and now you're gonna pay." Massacre.

14: And we thought the Book of Numbers was grandiose. Here 580,000 Judeans are said to fend off a million Ethiopians. Overhype much?

15: Random prophet appears to remind King Asa of the Chronicler's whole theme: seek G and live. Also, please kill any backsliders.

16: King Asa turns evil. He began so well, too; I had high hopes for this one. I need to stop getting emotionally invested.

17: King Jehoshaphat, aka "Phat," is blessed with riches and military might. He'll keep them as long as he's righteous . . . oh, damn.

18: On the eve of Phat's great battle he decides to ask G if the war is a good idea. It might have been prudent to ask BEFORE.

19: Phat's learned to trust G; installs Levitical judges through the land to teach people the law. But will the Senate confirm them?

20: Just when you think it's safe to retire in peace, your enemies gang up to attack you from the East. It's always something.

21: King Jehoram kills 6 brothers to grab the throne, but G can't ice him because of some old covenant. Gives him diarrhea though. So there.

22: Remember in the 10 Commandments when G said to obey Mom? Well, ignore that in this case. Ahaziah's ma is way, way wicked.

23: Athaliah becomes Judah's first and only ruling queen. She has ice for blood; executes the royal family. Like QE1, but even more badass.

24: King Joash turns wicked (don't they all?) and kills the prophet Zechariah, who dared to point out a few minor shortcomings.

25: Um, King Amaziah, if the Edomites' gods were so puny that you easily crushed them in battle, why would you now worship those gods?

26: G gives King Uzziah leprosy for making an offering in the temple. Fool, that's the Levites' job. And they're unionized.

27: Finally, we get a righteous king. It's about freakin' time. But good kings are boring, so this is the shortest chapter.

28: King Ahaz sells tickets to the Baal Ball. Come one, come all! The main event is child sacrifice, though, so don't sample the punch.

29: King Hezekiah does a massive spring cleaning in the temple. Out with the new, in with the old. Bye-bye, Baal: back to basics.

30: Hey, remember that Passover thing from Exodus? Let's, like, totally do that. With matzoh ball soup and bitter herbs and all. You in?

31: People are so generous in giving food to the temple priests that Hez organizes a trip to the Container Store for extra storage bins.

32: Judah has a pleasant *schadenfreude* moment as Israel gets pummeled by Assyria. We'd never say "We told you so," infidels, but . . . .

33: King Manasseh sows wild oats with foreign gods before a 180-degree conversion. G lets him off the hook. Nice guy, that G. Sometimes.

34: King Josiah does a national purge: No idols, high places, or sacred poles. Blue plaid ephods could also go. I'm just sayin'.

35: Josiah is slain by Pharaoh Neco, aka Necco Wafer. All Judah mourns and Jeremiah offers a special lament. He's famous for his laments.

36: Last chapter of Chronicles features young people hacked to bits, Jerusalem seized, and exile imminent. Hey, where's my happy ending?

If Israel's Oppressed, It Must Be Tuesday

It's awfully confusing that the Israelites had so many enemies. It would be one thing if the Old Testament/Hebrew Bible were told in chronological order so we could move logically from one oppressive overlord to the next. But the Bible's books skip around quite a bit in time, so one minute it seems like Assyria is the bad guy, and then you turn around and it's Babylon, and then it's Assyria again, and then it's Persia. How are we supposed to keep all the invaders straight?

Here's a very rudimentary timeline to help. Emphasis on the very. But at least it can give you some idea of what we're looking at.

Century	Oppressor du Jour	Some places to find this in the Bible
1200s BCE	Egypt	Exodus
1100–1000s BCE	Philistines	Judges, Samuel
700s BCE	Assyria (Israelites taken captive in 722 BCE)	Hosea, Amos, Micah, and Isaiah 1-39
600s–mid-500s BCE	Babylon (Judeans exiled to Babylon in 587ish BCE)	Jeremiah, Lamentations, Ezekiel, Daniel , and (probably) Isaiah 40-66
530s–430s BCE	Persia	Ezra, Nehemiah, Haggai, Zechariah, Esther
300s BCE	Greece	Not in Old Testament
200s BCE	Syria and Egypt, who politely take turns pummeling Israel	Not in Old Testament
63 BCE and for centuries thereafter	Rome	Entire New Testament

EZRA

Overview: After decades of exile in stinkin' Babylon, we're home and rebuilding. Actually, those gardens in Babylon were nice . . . .

1: Kinder, gentler Persia ousts Babylon and releases the Jews. Why? Because G told them to, and when G speaks, even the barbarians listen.

2: List of returnees includes over 42,000 folks plus servants. Uh oh! Macauley ben-Culkin isn't on the list. Did we leave him home alone?

3: Old people get seriously weepy at the foundation dedication for the second temple. They remember the first one back in the day, see. Sob.

4: Yes, we received your application to help rebuild the temple and play in our sandbox, but your blood's impure. Denied.

Cyrus the Great. No, I Mean It.

Things were rotten for the Jews when the nasty Babylonians destroyed the Jerusalem temple and took Judah captive in the 590s and 580s BCE. The exiled Jews must have had mixed feelings when, some decades later, Babylon started having serious invasion issues of its own.

Should they do a happy dance now that God was dishing out a bit of dastardly payback to their worst enemy? Or should they cower in fear at this turn of events, wondering if the Persians who had just taken over Babylon would prove to be even more tyrannical than the devil they knew?

It turned out that Persia was a sweetheart compared to the other oppressors of the ancient world. The Persian emperor, Cyrus, actually let the Jews go home around 537 BCE. Not all of them chose to—Babylon seemed pretty civilized compared to the herculean task of rebuilding Jerusalem, a city many of them had never even seen—but it was nice to be free to make that choice all the same.

Cyrus permitted the Jews to resume their own religious practices rather than imposing his own tradition (Zoroastrianism), and even kicked in money to rebuild the Jerusalem temple—a policy continued by his successor Darius. Considering that it had been the Babylonians and not the Persians who razed the temple in the first place, this was a generous gesture. The Book of Ezra says that Cyrus rummaged through the palace basement and found all the loot that the Babylonians had removed from the Jerusalem temple half a century before. Persia gave it all back: silver and gold basins, knives, bowls, and other shiny objects used for sacrificing animals on the altar.

Cyrus earned his honorific title "the Great" by being about 84 percent awesome. He was still an emperor, so it could never be 100 percent, but still. Gold star.

5: Oh crap. We can't find that old building-permit-edict-thingy from Cyrus. Construction workers play canasta till it turns up.

6: Darius not only allows the rebuilding of the Jewish temple; he foots the bill and even adds in a few Persian rugs as a goodwill gesture.

7: Ezra does double duty as Jerusalem's priest and scribe. But he's not too busy to also serve as acting mayor. What an overachiever.

8: Most Levites prefer being second-class citizens in Babylon to second-class citizens at home, even when Ezra promises 40 acres and a mule.

9: Confronted with the problem of foreign wives, Ezra prays, mourns, and appoints a committee to study the issue. Very Presbyterian.

10: Ezra's prayer moves the people to oust foreign wives. You'd think that a people so recently exiled themselves might be more sympathetic?

NEHEMIAH

Overview: The Engineers' Bible. We CAN rebuild it. We have the technology. Jerusalem will be better, stronger, faster, and more bionic.

1: Praying Nehemiah weeps at the idea of a scorched Jerusalem. Vows to become Rebuilderman action hero, sans cape. Capes are vain.

2: Neh inspects ruins of destroyed walls and gates. He wants to fix it all, especially Dung Gate. Because poop happens, even in the Bible.

3: New city will have Sheep Gate, Fish Gate, Old Gate, Valley Gate . . . wait, I thought we wanted to be LESS welcoming to attackers?

4: Every good building project will attract its share of protesters. Neh puts half of construction crew on guard duty. Take that, naysayers!

5: [Author query: This chapter is out of place here. Would you consider moving it after ch 13 for better flow? Thx. –Bible Editors.]

A Slow Rebuilding

The original manuscripts of the Bible have Ezra-Nehemiah as a single book, which makes sense since they both deal with rebuilding Jerusalem after the exile. Note, though, that it's not like Cyrus issued his liberating decree in the 530s and the captive Israelites all high-tailed it immediately back to their homeland. As we've already seen, some of them chose to stay behind and continue life in Babylon-now-Persia. (That is the setting of the book of Esther, for example.) Biblical scholar Mark Throntweit says,

> Many had learned to cope and even thrive in the environs of Mesopotamia and so were unwilling to pull up stakes and return to the impoverished conditions of Palestine. That the priestly families comprised a disproportionate ten percent of those who returned is a sobering testimony to the numbers who chose to stay behind. Especially ill-represented were Levites who may have felt they had little to gain in a secondary role in the Jerusalem temple.

As well, some of those families that did come back took their sweet time in doing so. Ezra-Nehemiah is set about eight decades after Cyrus's edict; Ezra made the trip down to Jerusalem in 458 BCE. John Goldingay points out that it's therefore not accurate to call Ezra a "hero of the return from the exile," since he would have been born decades after the exile ended. When he arrived in Jerusalem, the reconstruction of the temple was already underway, the pet project of some early returnees and the many residents of Judah who were never carted off to Babylon in the first place.

Still, Ezra's contribution was of great symbolic importance, not just in rebuilding the temple but in refocusing the people's attention back to the Torah, the first five books of the Bible. Ezra and Nehemiah wanted to return Israelites to a strict monotheism and adherence to the law, meaning that they had to banish all their foreign wives, stop charging each other interest for loans, keep the Sabbath holy, etc. Like many instances of biblical reform, Ezra and Nehemiah's ideal Torah society didn't last; people tend to return to their wicked ways sooner rather than later.

6: Protesters step it up. Not just "Builders Go Home" signs now, but death threats. Something there is that doesn't love a wall.

7: New city walls are finished in just 52 days! Nehemiah & Co get A+ rating on Angie's List for stonemasonry. Sermons at no extra charge.

8: Governor Neh has Ezra the priest read the law out loud to the people, who burst into tears. Torah has that effect sometimes.

9: Day of national confession. People repent for idol worship, blasphemy, killing prophets, and listening to Lady Gaga on their iPods.

10: People take remedial Covenant 101 course because they flunked the first 22,000 times. Keep the law; don't forget G. HOW HARD IS THAT?

11: Lottery for "town mouse, country mouse." Only 10% of folks get to live in Jerusalem. Other 90% pull *Green Acres* and bad teeth.

12: Heyheyhey, Part-ay! People play Twister on new walls at dedication celebration. Watch where you step at Dung Gate, though.

13: FYI, the city gates will be closed from sundown Fri to sundown Sat. In case you were planning to sell fish or wine then . . . just don't.

ESTHER

Overview: Thrilling novel about a Fifth Column in the Persian court. One of 2 books in Bible not to mention G, who's offstage w/ cue cards.

1: Queen Vashti refuses to appear in court swimsuit competition, which deflates the king's supersized ego. She gets a pink slip . . . NEXT!

2: Orphaned Jew Esther gets a year of spa treatments and wins beauty pageant to wed the king. He is still a jerk, but it's a fairy tale.

3: Enter villain Haman Hitler, king's second-in-command, who wants to wipe out all Jews in Persia. Boo! Hiss! Stomp your feet.

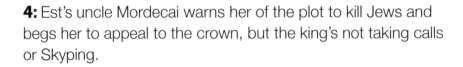

4: Est's uncle Mordecai warns her of the plot to kill Jews and begs her to appeal to the crown, but the king's not taking calls or Skyping.

5: The way to a king's ♥: Est plans a special feast. But Haman's building gallows for Jews, so hurry w/ the girly banquet prep, OK?

6: King gives Uncle Mord the royal treatment after learning he once saved the day. Haman seethes with jealousy: "Darn those Jews!"

7: The feast's a smashing success and the king grants Est's wish to save the Jews. Villain Haman also being at banquet table? AWKward.

8: Haman is hoisted by his own petards! Mord gets his job; Est gets his house; Jews get excuse to always drink on Purim. A win-win.

9: King can't reverse his own decree to kill Jews, but allows them to defend themselves against attack. A happy bloodbath ensues. Thx, Est!

10: Anticlimactic chapterlet to say that A) Uncle Mord grew very powerful in the Persian court; and B) don't mess with Jews. Esther ends.

JOB

Overview: I'd tell you about Job, but man, my boils are itchy. Also, my kids all snuffed it and G's gone AWOL. Waaaaah. Why me? *Why?*

1: "The Satan" makes Bible debut; looks Job up on "The Google." Is Job really that pious? Let's kill his 10 kids and find out!

2: Job still won't curse G, so Satan ups the ante by giving Job boils on his skin. Surely now the guy will crack. Literally.

3: Now entering 40+ chapters of poetry. Job curses the day he was born—with onomatopoeia, no less. That's grace under pressure.

4: With friends like these, who needs Friends of Job? FOJ #1 says, "Dude, this is all your fault. You reap what you sow."

5: FOJ #1 cont: "Happy are those the Lord disciplines!" That's easy for you to say, Mr. Smug. You're not childless and covered in boils.

6: Job: "Gee, did you also bring salt and lemon to rub into my open sores, here, people? Talk about blaming the victim. Sheesh."

7: Job talks to G like his friends aren't really there. (They never listen anyway, so it's OK.) "G, just let me croak already."

8: FOJ #2 insists that good people always get rewarded and bad people always get punished. He learned that at the movies.

9: Job: "Once more for the hearing impaired: I'm *blameless*. Really. This isn't punishment for sin!" But FOJs don't get the memo.

10: Job: "Woe is me. G, I'm hauling your ass to court for abandonment. My life sucks and it's not my fault. *Where's Judge Judy?*"

11: FOJ #3 tells Job to stop blaspheming and start IDing where he sinned. If he repents, everything will be peachy again. Promise!

12: Job belts a 12-bar blues classic about being a laughingstock, but follows up with a praise song about G's terrible power. Kinda schizo.

13: Job: "OK, that's it. I'm lawyering up. But you 3 clowns will NOT represent me with your cute aphorisms. The door is that way."

14: Deep Thoughts about death: We're like those leaves that trickle down, always at the mercy of the Great Leaf Blower of life.

15: FOJ #1: "Job, you're undermining Mom, religion, tradition, and green bean casserole. You make me nervous with your questions."

16: Job: "Can I just say that you 3 stink as comforters? You talk, talk, talk, but do you even care? Wait, don't answer that."

17: Job prays to G for relief from suffering. It might also be nice if G saw fit to smite his so-called friends. Just an idea.

18: FOJ #2 strains his head with this syllogism: "If G punishes the wicked, and Job is suffering, THEREFORE Job is wicked. It's so clear."

19: Job: "I know that my avenger lives. It'd be gratifying if I got justice before my flesh is ripped off, but I guess I can't be picky."

20: FOJ #3 starts getting all offended and reminds Job that the wicked never go unpunished. Job is rolling what remains of his eyes.

21: Job: "Actually, wickedness goes unpunished often. Exhibit A is standing here in front of me. Remind me why you're still here, liar?"

22: And it's Round 3 with the 3 FOJs! FOJ #1 goes for the jugular and says Job oppressed widows and the poor. Them's fightin' words.

23: Job mutters to G about how an upright person who obeyed the law ought to be permitted to lodge a proper complaint. So there.

24: Q: Why does Donald Trump prosper and celebrities go free after murder? *Why,* G? A: Um, we'll get back to you on that. Or not.

25: FOJ #2 finally says something worth hearing: "Job, G is all-powerful, and YOU'RE NOT HIM." Well, when you put it that way.

26: Job: "Again with the blame-the-victim schtick. But since you mention it, G *is* pretty amazing, huh? Who are we to understand?"

27: Death comes even to the rich. This is a good thing, or there'd be no justice at all. When it does, can I take your vineyard?

28: We've had a lot of heavy philosophy, so let's interrupt with a lovely song to Dame Wisdom, who rocks. Gold and silver can't equal her.

29: Job offers closing argument as his own defense counsel: "My life used to be so blessed. I helped the poor. WTF happened, G?"

30: Job: "Now I'm mocked and hated; why? And why is G not answering my calls? Oh, and my skin is falling off. What's up with THAT?"

31: Job ends closing argument and insists he's blameless. What judge wouldn't be moved by his ordeal? Judge G, it seems. *Silence.*

 J o b **111**

Wisdom Literature

The Bible is one wise book. Well, actually, the Bible is a compilation of many wise books, written by many people over the course of centuries. But some of those books are wiser than others, and those are the ones called "wisdom literature." (Cryptic, I know. Stay with me.)

Let's take a look at where this wisdom lit fits into the grand scheme of the Bible. In the Old Testament/Hebrew Bible, the three main divisions of books are:

1. **Torah, or the Pentateuch.** The Torah (Hebrew for "law") is made up of the first five books of the Bible. As you probably remember, it's mostly history with some important laws thrown in, like the one about washing hands over a dead cow whenever you're trying to figure out who committed a murder (Deut. 21). This vital crime-solving technique is now standard procedure in our nation's police academies.

2. **Nevi'im, or the Prophets.** We've already seen some of these books, called the "Former Prophets" (Joshua, Judges, 1 and 2 Samuel, and 1 and 2 Kings). Pretty soon we'll get to the really juicy "Latter Prophets," like Isaiah, Jeremiah, and Ezekiel. They have some, er, lively words to tell Israel about the many inventive ways God is planning to carve her up and serve her to Assyria. Or maybe Babylon. Or perhaps Persia.

3. Ketuvim, or the Writings. Every taxonomic system needs a catch-all category, right? Well, "the Writings" would be it for the Bible. This includes everything from history (the Ezra-Nehemiah unit and Chronicles) to wisdom literature, which gets its name not just from its sage advice (though there's that), but also because Dame Wisdom often appears in these books as a personified character. In the Bible, wisdom starts with standing in awe of God (Prov. 9:10), so it's more about putting God first than it is about accumulating degrees or particular knowledge. The wisdom literature books include:

- Job
- Psalms
- Proverbs
- Ecclesiastes
- Song of Solomon
- A couple of other books that Protestants have downgraded to the Apocrypha but which you should check out anyway

A primary feature of the Bible's wisdom literature is poetry, which is a significant portion of the Book of Job here. Remember that you get extra credit as a *Twible* reader every time you go back to the original Bible for a consult, and that's especially true of the wisdom literature. The poetry is often gorgeous, and 140 characters can't even begin to do it justice.

32: Job gets the champion he's been seeking in young Elihu, who makes mincemeat of the FOJs' arguments. Hooray! An eleventh-hour witness!

33: Hold the phone. Elihu's rebuking Job now too: "G's bigger than any human, even a Mr. Clean type like you." Things get interesting.

34: Elihu turns out not to be Job's defense attorney so much as G's Piety Czar. Rats. Job knew he should've hired Dershowitz.

35: Elihu: "Let's get some perspective. G's a lot bigger than you, Job. Try to see his side, and don't be such a Debbie Downer."

36: Elihu insists that G is fair, despite Job's dead kids, rotting body, and sudden famine. For some reason, Job's not feeling the love.

37: Elihu closes his speech with a nod to G's impressive natural wonders. Thunderbolt and lightning, very very frightening. Be afraid.

38: G makes an unexpected cameo appearance, going mano-a-mano with Job about creation: "Where were you, punk, when I created the earth?"

39: G goes at Job again with the 20 Questions about creation. Bottom line: If you want to play God, you first need to be a top veterinarian.

The Friends of Job

I've been a little hard on the FOJs (Friends of Job) in these tweets. In condemning them I'm standing in a long line of interpreters who sniff and say, "Some friends!" every time one of the companions says something stupid, which is often. We like to see ourselves as Job—wrongly accused, shattered by loss, deserving of sympathy—but not in the characters of his several friends.

But philosopher Mark Larrimore cautions in *The Book of Job: A Biography* that this is a misleading path for us to take. "The book of Job should teach us to expect failures of friendship, especially from ourselves," he says. Even though Job's friends seem to continually say the wrong things, blaming Job for his suffering and clinging to conventional pieties, Larrimore points out that there's no textual evidence the three clowns ever leave his side. By the end Job may have *wanted* them to leave his side, but they probably didn't. And that in itself is friendship—even while they spout platitudes or shrink from his deep and discomfiting theological questions, they're still accompanying him in his misery. Like the friends, Larrimore says that we, too, should keep company with Job, recognizing that "Job's questions are not only 'unfinalized' but 'unfinalizable.'" Our obligation is to listen to the pain.

40: Job: "Uh, sorry. It seems I'm out of my league." G: "We're not finished. You called me down here and now we're gonna RUMBLE."

41: G: "And have you met my pet Leviathan? No, I didn't THINK so. If you can't even face him, why would you want to mess with me?"

42: Justice. G rebukes the FOJs; restores Job's kids and wealth. But being G means never having to say you're sorry. Where's Ms. Manners?

PSALMS

Overview: Israel's top 150 countdown. Songs for all: sad ballads, joyful praises, and foul curses for your worst bullies on the playground.

1: G pens the self-help bestseller *Live Long and Prosper.* Spoiler: one key to happiness is to buy all of G's books. So now you know.

2: G says David's his son and the chosen king. Those other kings, G just laughs at. Before he roasts them. G can be testy that way.

3: G will smite our enemies and break the teeth of the wicked. This psalm explains a lot about dentistry in the biblical world.

4: For insomniacs. If you're upset, 1) stay in bed; 2) count sheep; and 3) sacrifice the sheep. This works even better than warm milk.

5: Please, G, rain down karmic retribution upon my enemies. Just this once, and I'll never ask for anything again. Not even a pony.

6: G, I cry in my sleep every night. Since a sopping, snotty pillow is unhygienic, can you please start answering my text messages?

7: A "Shiggaion" of David = a wild ballad enhanced by strong emotion and perhaps even stronger libation. Way to go meshugah, baby.

8: Yo, G! The moon and stars you made are, like, WOW. People must be disappointing by comparison. How come you never give up on us?

9: Thx, G, for destroying the wicked and saving the poor. But can you hurry up the justice thing a little? No pressure, but . . .

10: G, bring that giant ear closer to earth to hear the cries of those in pain. You *are* going to smite the wicked, right? And soon?

11: G will rain fire and sulfur on the wicked, and there won't even be enough evil folk left to make a reality show about it on MTV.

12: A Psalm according to the Sheminith. I could tell you what a Sheminith is, but the word sounds way cooler with a little mystery.

13: Where r u, G? I've been looking all over. R u dissing me? My life sucks. I need to vent, & u r AWOL. Some friend. How long?

14: Fools say in their hearts that there is no God. G retorts that basically everyone's an idiot. G's in one of his moods, see.

The Cursing Psalms

The Psalter has a number of different kinds of songs—worship, praise, lament, and a polka thrown in for good measure. But what could be more fun than composing songs about your enemies' destruction?

Called the psalms of imprecation, these songs call on God to harm, maim, or even kill our enemies. It's no wonder that the psalms of imprecation are often mysteriously absent from lectionary cycles and sermon plans.

While I think that Psalm 137 is the worst, C.S. Lewis gave that dubious honor to Psalm 109, and after rereading it I can see his point.

When he is tried, let him be found guilty;
   let his prayer be counted as sin.
May his days be few;
   may another seize his position.
May his children be orphans,
   and his wife a widow.
May his children wander about and beg;
   may they be driven out of the ruins they inhabit.
May the creditor seize all that he has;
   may strangers plunder the fruits of his toil.
May there be no one to do him a kindness,
   nor anyone to pity his orphaned children. (Ps. 109:7-12)

Whichever psalm packs the most imprecatory punch, one thing is certain: these songs, for better or for worse, are part of the canon. They represent an ugly part of the human experience, but they are human nonetheless.

Still, I wouldn't recommend belting them out at church or synagogue anytime soon.

15: G's peeps are honest (✓), hate evil (✓), and don't slam their neighbors (✓). They also never lend money at interest. Oops.

16: Ad: "The lines have fallen for me in pleasant places" because I use G's own facial cream. It's bracing on my skin, but effective.

17: Hide me in the shadow of your wings, G. They're even cozier than goose down, and they don't hurt the environment. Love that.

18: Long and trippy psalm about G's badass warrior days. Smoke even came from his nostrils. Do they make holy Kleenex for that?

19: "Heaven's telling the glory of God…" So *that's* what heaven's saying. I have AT&T, see. It kept dropping heaven's calls.

20: May G grant your ♥'s desire and fulfill all your plans. Except that scheme about meeting Angelina Jolie. Give it up, man.

21: Righteous monarchs get blessings and a long reign. Well, not Lady Jane Grey. Her 9-day reign didn't end well. But OTHERWISE . . . .

22: My God, my God, why have you forsaken me? Was it the onions I ate? Or maybe the beans? I knew I should've avoided the beans.

23: G's my shepherd. He lets me nap in green pastures. He protects me from the wolves. Sometimes it rocks to be a sheep, y'know?

24: "Lift up your heads, O gates! Be lifted up, O ancient doors!" Yes, it's an odd metaphor. It's poetry. Work with me, people.

25: Don't remember the sins of my youth, G. Especially that one time when we were all baking rum cake at the frat house. OK? Thx!

26: A Psalm for hypocrites. "Don't hose me, G. I did what you asked and didn't sit with those losers at lunch. I'm righteous! I'm holy! I—"

27: G's my personal nightlight; whom shall I fear? I'll be fine in war. Or if enemies eat my flesh. On second thought . . . eeeww.

28: Payback time for the wicked—or at least, we hope so. Break 'em down, move 'em out. Go ahead, G. Make. Their. Day.

29: If you can't beat the Canaanites, you can at least steal their best tunes. This rockin' ode to Baal got an extreme makeover.

30: G turned my mourning into dancing. He's not a very predictable *DWTS* partner for waltzing, though. Better for . . . the tango!

31: Into your hands I commend my spirit, G. Please have it cryogenically frozen until such time as life is not so freakin' harsh.

32: Finally confessed the thing I did that time. You know what I mean, G. Glad I got THAT off my chest. Let's be transparent more often.

33: G is both great and good, despite what Christopher Hitchens said. So we'll sing to G a new song. Like, say, this psalm here.

34: The righteous suffer afflictions, but G will rescue them. Well, that's a relief because I was starting to worry. Anytime now, G.

35: G, please kick the asses of my enemies. Don't hold back. Stab 'em with the spear, then the javelin. That's the ticket.

36: The wicked imagine that all their dark deeds are in secret. We've got news for you: @GInHvn just posted them on Twitter. Ha!

37: The meek will inherit the land that was fertilized by the decomposing bodies of the wicked. It's poetic justice, if a bit gross.

38: Symptoms: open sores, numbness, dizziness, back pain. Huh, G? You say my sin caused this? Oh, sure. Attribution FAIL.

39: Well, shut my mouth! No, really—do actually shut it. It keeps getting me in trouble. And if you can't say anything nice . . .

40: I'm glad that burnt offering thing is in the past. Sacrifices were so gross. But writing the law on my heart? Harder than it looks.

41: Even my best friend pulled a Judas on me. Sheesh, you can't trust anyone nowadays. At least my homeboy G's got my back.

The Full Spectrum of Human Emotion

Peter Gomes, the late minister of Harvard's Memorial Church, used to direct people to the Psalms whenever they would come to him wondering how they should begin reading the Bible. He would suggest starting not with Genesis but with these 150 songs, which represent the full spectrum of human emotion and experience.

In her book *The Psalms*, Kathleen Norris tells Gomes's story and agrees that the Psalms are a fine starting place because they are "blessedly untidy." Their wide range of expression, which includes imprecation and praise and lament and confession, "allows us to bring our whole lives before God." She writes:

> The realism of the Psalms flies in the face of much contemporary spirituality that presupposes a golden age in the past to which only the enlightened may aspire in the present. In the Psalms we find a more genuine continuity with our human past. I find it oddly refreshing that as ancient as they are the Psalms reflect our world as it is, full of violence, greed, and betrayal: "Yea, mine own familiar friend, in whom I trusted, which did eat of my bread, hath lifted up his heel against me' (Ps. 41:9) . . . . In Psalms such as these, as C.S. Lewis has noted in his *Reflections on the Psalms*, "No historical readjustment is required. We are in the world we know."
>
> Thankfully, we are also in a world we do not know. One in which pretense is stripped away, and even the worst human emotions—jealousy or the desire for vengeance—are not denied or hidden, but brought into the open and put before God. This is what makes the Psalter a truly holy book, and also what makes us squirm.

42: As the deer longs for the water, so my soul longs after you. And if you could include a salt lick, that would be extra special.

43: "Why are you cast down, O my soul? And why am I talking to myself? Must be the stress of enemies plotting my death and all."

44: G, our ancestors told us what a kick-ass deity you are, but what have you done for us lately? We're dyin' here. Wake up, dude!

45: Ode for a royal wedding! The only love song in the Psalter. And Kate, you have to promise to obey your master William. Right.

46: G is our refuge and strength, a very present help in times of trouble. So no matter what, don't be afraid. Just be chillaxin.

47: Get on your feet, people! Clap your hands for G's unsurpassed awesomeness. Sing and shout. Come on, I can't HEAR you . . . .

48: Jerusalem may in reality be a backwater town, but it's *our* backwater town, and G's favorite hangout. So there.

49: Don't be sad when others get rich, or win the HGTV dream house. They're all gonna die someday. Death is the great equalizer.

50: G: "Don't give me no bull, Israel. Why did you think I'd be appeased by animal sacrifice? Really, just say thx. Maybe with chocolate."

51: "I sinned and I'm extra sorry. Here's my broken spirit. I would have killed you a goat, but I hear you don't like those anymore."

52: The righteous will one day taunt wicked sinners in their best Church Lady voices. Now isn't that special?

53: Fools say in their hearts, "There is no God." G says in his heart, "Dang! I sure did manufacture an awful lot of fools."

54: Choirmasters, be sure to sing this with stringed instruments, or else people won't get the full effect of all the whining. Thx.

55: Fear, trembling, dread, horror. This is one of those 3 A.M. psalms for comfort after a nightmare. Or a Wes Craven movie.

56: Crush my enemies and make them into jam. I'll spread them on toast and eat them at tea. Or maybe put them in donuts. Mmm, enemy donuts.

57: My soul is between the lions, and not in a nice *PBS Kids* way. I think these lions may have skipped breakfast. Oh dear.

58: Let my enemies be like the snail that dissolves into slime. I've never actually seen that happen, but it FEELS like justice.

59: G, don't just kill my enemies; fight them to the pain. Leave them in anguish, wallowing in freakish misery forever. Yesssss.

60: G promised he'd hurl his shoe at Edom, and in Middle Eastern cultures that's not a good thing. So why'd they flog us in battle?

Who Wrote the Psalms?

As you read the Psalms, you'll notice that each song has a prologue of sorts with instructions to the music leader. ("Set to rap beat" is a common directive.) You'll also see that approximately half of the psalms are said to be "of David."

Traditionally, many people have interpreted this to mean that David actually wrote all those psalms himself. After all, the Bible notes his musical skill at the lyre (1 Sam. 16:17); when young David played for King Saul, Saul could forget his worries for a while.

The problem is with a Hebrew preposition that can mean *of* but also *to, from, according to*, or *for*. It's all a bit loosey-goosey. The Psalms could have been written by David, or they could have been written by court musicians in David's honor. Many were also likely composed decades or even centuries after his death. Having his name attached to these songs was considered a compliment; the ancient world wasn't as hung up as we are on things like copyright and iTunes royalties.

It's entirely possible that David wrote a psalm or two himself. I, for one, would like to think he penned Psalm 51 and really did feel that guilty about shacking up with a married woman and then offing her spouse.

However, it's highly unlikely that David wrote every psalm that is attributed to him. After all, he was a busy king with Philistines to slaughter.

Are You There, God?
It's Me, the Psalmist

- "How long?" (Ps. 13:1)
- "Every night I flood my bed with tears." (Ps. 6:6)
- "I am persecuted without cause; help me!" (Ps. 119:86)
- "O Lord, make haste to help me!" (Ps. 70:1)

Anyone who spends time reading the Psalms understands that this is the part of the Bible where the Shiny Happy Fallacy crumbles apart; real faith involves serious questions and doubts, and is not satisfied by platitudes. There's a world of suffering in these pages, as well as hope and praise.

The Psalms are for everybody who's ever wondered where God is when bad things happen to good people. They're for people who question how long it will take for God to get off his ass and stop their suffering. And they're for you, whenever you feel abandoned and alone.

Some people feel guilty even for experiencing those emotions, or for expressing sadness or anger to God. If this is you, it might be good to take a look at what Jesus said when he was dying on the cross, discarded by his disciples and friends. He quoted Psalm 22: "My God, my God, why have you forsaken me?" (Ps. 22:1). It's worth noting that even though Jesus was not actually abandoned by God, he clearly felt that way at the time, and the words he chose to express that isolation were ones that had been consecrated by centuries of prayer.

61: Lead me to the rock that is higher. Just leave me a rope ladder so I can still climb down after my religious high.

62: For G alone my soul waits in silence. He's running late, but my soul waits in silence. This is me, being silent. Out loud.

63: G, you're water in the desert to me. I can't help falling in love with you. Have I told you lately that I love you? At last . . .

64: My enemies whet their tongues like swords. They aim bitter words like arrows. But hey, I still rule in the simile department.

65: Thanksgiving Psalm. G waters the earth, provides us with grain, and crowns us with bounty. Please pass the yams, rolls, and pie.

66: G, you put us thru hell, stomped on us, and let our enemies triumph. But we deserved all that. SO glad you still love us.

67: G's so amazing that it's a mystery why all the nations around us don't fall down in worship. Give it up for our G, Egypt!

68: Loooong Ps; basic message is this: Hang with mobster G. He'll split our enemies' heads open and break their kneecaps. Yay!

69: G, I know you don't really want my enemies to triumph here. It would make you look like a total wuss deity. Man up, please.

70: O Lord, make haste to help me. Just FYI, "haste" means "hurry." As in, step on it. Now. Do not pass go. Do not collect $200.

71: Even to old age and grey hairs, do not forsake me. Even to lumbago and arthritis and dementia. Even to incontinence. Wait, TMI.

72: G, please help our king Solomon, so that he'll deliver the needy when they call. And not enslave them. Slavery would be a bummer.

73: You know, the wicked don't seem to be doing so badly. They're gorgeous and wealthy and praised. Remind me why that is?

74: Rise up, G, and plead the cause of the poor. They couldn't afford a lawyer and you've been appointed as Public Defender #1.

75: When earthquakes come, both literal and metaphorical, G will keep us steady. Except for the wicked, who are once again toast.

76: G, everyone is terrified of you. It's that awful temper of yours! Thx for throwing stuff at our enemies this time though.

77: I'm trying to remind myself of those great deeds you did in the past, G, because right now I'm sad and exhausted. You still with me?

78: This gives G's side of the story, and is HE ever ticked. Sees himself as a Giving Tree that Israel keeps lifting its leg to pee on.

79: G, pour out your anger on the nations who don't know you, not at us. We're family! Go pick on some goyim for a change.

80: G, you're supposed to be a shepherd, right? So herd us right back to you. Please don't make us into mutton pie for our enemies.

81: In which G plays the role of the mother no one appreciates. "No, don't mind me. I'll just sit here alone in the dark."

82: G convenes an international welfare summit with other gods. Baal fattens up on donuts while G advocates enhancing Medicaid programs.

83: Kick our enemies' butts like you did to those Midianites that time with all the blood and guts and gore. That was our *favorite*.

84: I'd rather be a doorkeeper in the temple of my G than dwell with you fools in Disney's Magic Kingdom. But maybe I'll visit.

85: How long will you be ticked at us, G? Cause this time-out chair is hard and uncomfortable. We'll be good now, we promise. Please, Daddy?

86: G, I've been your faithful follower all my life and now it's payback time. You totally owe me. So go shame my foes ASAP.

87: Quick! Provide long-form proof that you were native-born in Jerusalem and are registered in G's Book of Zion. Cough it up.

88: Only Psalm without even the pretense of a happy ending: Life sucks and then you die. So why is this one of my favorite Psalms?

89: Why would you create me just so my foes can Slushie me? Will you hide yourself forever? I'm not getting any younger here.

90: Teach us to number our days. Also, make us glad for every single day you've punished us. We're learning a lot from it, really.

91: G's CV says he'll deliver, cover, protect, answer, rescue, and extend life. With action verbs like that he should be CEO Deity!

92: It is good to give thanks to G. We're not like those eejits who can't appreciate anything. They are such losers.

93: G is the king over all creation, in case you missed it. Not Elvis. Not Michael Jackson. Not even Budweiser.

94: Yo, God of vengeance! You say that those you discipline will be happy. Please, make my enemies *fantastically* happy. Today.

95: Kneel before Zod. I mean, God. Don't be stubborn like that time at Massah in the wilderness. That did not end well, people.

96: Sing, sing, sing! Tell all the good stuff that G's done. P.S. Ocean, sky, and fields: be sure to join in the chorus, OK?

97: In case you imagined from the last few happy Psalms that G was a sweet-little-pushover-Grandma-styled god, think FIRE. Oh.

The Beauty of Psalm 88

It's hard to make jokes about Psalm 88, so I won't even try. But I will tell you it's among my favorite psalms. Why? Because it tells it like it is.

Psalm 88 is easily the most depressing piece of poetry in the Psalter. Sure, other psalms start out whining about this or that—maybe the psalmist is sick, or wondering why God hasn't shown up to fix things already, or has been ridiculed by enemies. Sometimes those tirades can be pretty harsh, and the psalmist lets God have it in no uncertain terms. But those poems always end with some kind of affirmation of faithfulness along the lines of, "Yes, my life completely sucks right now, but I will trust in God's steadfast love! He hasn't let me down yet! The sun'll come out tomorrow!"

Not so Psalm 88, and that is why it's special. It simply ends mid-rant in what translator Robert Alter calls "utter darkness." Eighty-eight is a bleak, austere Psalm, but my life is better just knowing that it's there, part of the canon, its darkness ameliorating my darkness.

I am reminded of a time when I got to interview Martin Marty, a prominent scholar of American religion, about a book he had written. He told me that when his wife was dying, they had a practice of reading the Psalms together every night. "I'd get up with her at midnight when she took her medication and we would read the Psalms," he told me. "I would read the even numbered Psalms and she would read the odds. I skipped 88 and she caught me. She said, 'Who do you think you are to skip that? If you don't pray the rough ones, the other ones don't mean anything.'"

I loved that. We are called to pray Psalm 88 exactly because it's desolate and terrifying. God is there, part of the darkness. This Psalm's presence in the Bible means that no matter what we are facing, God can take our howls about the pain without our having to sugarcoat it.

98: Let the rivers clap their hands. Afterwards, please stop taking the hallucinogens that caused you to see rivers clapping.

99: G's enthroned upon his cherubim. They considered complaining about being badly squashed like that, but they're too cherubic.

100: Worship checklist: make joyful noise, worship, come, know, enter, give thx, and bless. Gosh. Happy people have a lot to remember.

101: The king will be a Boy Scout, practicing integrity, good deeds, and honesty. Oh, and eviscerating the wicked with a Swiss Army knife.

102: I'm deathly ill, groaning in the night like a lost owl. I'll wither like grass, but G'll last forever. It's an odd comfort.

103: "Bless the Lord, O my soul!" Did you realize when your granny said that, she was actually quoting the Psalms? Who knew?

104: Israel's version of Egypt's Top 40 "Hymn to the Aten," their sun god. But G's lord over sun AND moon AND stars. Top that, Egypt.

105: Did you doze through the Bible's first pages? No worries, mate, because it's all here in miniature: *Genesis & Exodus for Dummies.*

106: Q: Who can utter the Lord's mighty acts? A: Our Psalmist, apparently, who then does so for 48 verses. The takeaway: G rules.

107: Book 5 begins. I kind of forgot to tell you that the Psalms are divided into 5 books. Twibling is complicated.

108: G, remember when you used to go out into battle with us? How come you don't do that anymore? Get down here with your badass self.

109: Bible's worst curses: "May your penis be fruitless! May a bank foreclose! May you die young!" Tell us how you really feel.

110: G promises he will make footstools out of our enemies. We can even have them reupholstered to match our chosen décor.

111: An acrostic poem. A: G's adorable. B: G's so Beautiful. C: He's a Cutie! And D: Delightful. You see where this is going.

All God's Critters Gotta Sing in the Choir

There are happy songs mixed all throughout the Psalter, but if you read the whole collection straight through you'll be struck by how many of them fall in the last third or so. And while a lot of Psalms—especially the ones about suffering—focus on human experiences, plenty of others cast a broader net, asking all of creation to join in the act of praising God. In Psalm 98, for example, we've got rivers clapping their hands with joy and even some hills singing—and this is nearly three thousand years before *The Sound of Music*. In Psalm 96 the sea roars its praise, paving the way for Psalm 148, when the sea monsters chime in. You kind of want to be a safe distance away when that happens.

The basic idea is that everything God has created—everything that has breath, and even a lot of things that don't—will exalt the name of the Lord.

112: G's followers bless others. They prosper, but they help the poor. The wicked just gnash their teeth. What's the point of that?

113: G'll raise up the poor and let them sit with princes. He'll bless the infertile with kids. He's just taking his sweet time is all.

114: Exodus redux, with 'tude: "What's your issue, sea, that you run away from G? And you, river? You just can't take G, huh? *HUH?*"

115: Those idols you love can't compare to G up there in the heavens, Israel, so just WALK AWAY. That's right. You can do it.

116: Song of recovery from illness, depression, and/or despair. Insert your personal crisis here. Oh, and be sure to thank G.

117: Shortest Ps. *ALL* nations have to praise G because of what he did for Israel. We're talking to you, Egypt and Syria. PTL, already.

118: G's love endures forever. And ever. Hallelujah. Hallelujah. Now, go sing it at the mall and shock some total strangers.

119: Thy word is a lamp unto my feet. OK, but can't you use a super bright LED and not this lame flashlight with flaky batteries?

120: First of 15 Songs of Ascents. (No, it's not *that* kind of high. Just say no. It's about making a pilgrimage to Jerusalem.)

121: G's bodyguard firm advertises 24/7 protection: "He will not let your foot be moved! He who keeps you will not slumber!"

122: "Peace be within your walls, Jerusalem." Well, someday. Maybe. If you can get your crap together and stop warring. We'll see.

123: "Let us praise God. O Lord, You are so big, so absolutely huge. Gosh, we're all really impressed down here." –Monty Python

124: Thank G that G's on our side. If that isn't too tautological or anything. If it weren't for G, we'd be G-less.

125: G, do good to those who do good. Is that so hard? Life would be a lot less complicated if you'd just do this one thing for us.

The ABC Bible

One device of biblical poetry that doesn't usually come through in English translation is the "acrostic" style, which means that a piece of Hebrew writing—usually but not always a poem—is told alphabetically. If you think this sounds like kids' stuff, well, it is; the main focus of acrostic poetry is making Scripture easier to memorize.

While a number of Psalms employ this style (9, 10, 25, 37, 111, and 145, among others), the granddaddy of them all is Psalm 119. It is not only the longest Psalm but the longest chapter, bar none, in the whole Hebrew Bible. Each of the twenty-two letters of the Hebrew alphabet gets eight verses, making for a grand total of 176 lines of poetry in this Psalm. Whew. Good luck memorizing that one.

The acrostic device also crops up in Proverbs, like with the "Woman of Worth" in Proverbs 31. That Proverb makes it clear that she's awesome, bodacious, capable, dependable, efficient, fabulous, and . . . well, you get the idea. And for extra fun, almost the entire book of Lamentations is an extended alphabetical list of grievances.

Good times, good abecedarian times.

126: The slings and arrows of outrageous fortune have made mincemeat of us once again. Not to get all Shakespearean on you.

127: Blessed is the man who has a quiverful of sons. His ginormous family shall have joy and their very own reality show on TLC.

128: The man who fears G will have an über-fertile wife who stays in the back room pushing out more kids. Yep, sign me up for that.

129: May all who hate Zion be put to shame. Make them like thatch that withers on the rooftop. (Hey, good one. That'll show em.)

130: If you, G, should keep track of sin, who could stand? We'd be flunking out for sure. I already got a D in religion class.

131: My heart is not proud, G. I am never haughty. Except maybe now, when I'm explaining how very humble I am.

132: A gentle reminder, G: you promised to keep David's line on the throne. Remember? We're all getting a bit worried down here.

133: How pleasant it is when people dwell together in unity! We'll enjoy peace for the 5.3 seconds it lasts. And . . . cue fight scene.

134: 3-verse, all-purpose psalm: 1) Praise G. 2) Lift up your hands. 3) Be blessed. Would that religion were always this simple.

135: Other nations' idols are silver and gold, made by human hands. Idols = BAD. But gold = GOOD, so let's use it for a nice chalice!

136: This psalm informs us 26 different times that G's love endures forever. And we thought today's pop songs were repetitive.

137: Blessed is the one who can snatch up a sweet Babylonian baby and smash its brains against a rock. Cause G is all about that.

138: On the day I called, G answered me, and his right hand delivered me. G's left hand was out of the office on vacation as usual.

139: Wherever I go, G, you're always there with me. Kinda glad you're my own personal stalker, even to the outer limits of the sea.

140: Let burning coals rain down on my enemies! May they fall into a ravine! I'd dance a little jig. Just dreaming out loud here.

141: A psalm of David, which is a lot like the other psalms of David. Being king means never having to admit you're redundant.

Dashing Babies' Heads against a Rock, and Other Bible Fun

When I sent *The Twible* out for feedback from early readers before publication, one of the pastors who covered the Psalms section noted that Psalm 137 was the only one that she didn't find the least bit funny. She put it down to the "baby head-smashing thing" not being a terribly comical image.

I feel exactly the same way. Remember when we discussed the cursing Psalms, and I said that Psalm 137 is my nominee for the very worst, most unspeakable imprecation? That's because 137 imagines the unique joy that Israel will experience when it sees the infant children of its enemy Babylon being dashed against some rocks. Uh huh.

The setting for this let's-take-the-baby-out-of-Babylon Psalm is significant. This is an angry, miserable, exiled community that has just seen its home destroyed and can't find any joy or connection to God in their new circumstances. That setting may help explain such sick fantasies about wishing their enemies' infants to have their brains bashed in, but it does not excuse them. Here is what Robert Alter has to say:

> No moral justification can be offered for this notorious concluding line. All one can do is to recall the background of outraged feeling that triggers the conclusion: The Babylonians have laid waste to Jerusalem, exiled much of its population, looted and massacred; the powerless captives, ordered—perhaps mockingly—to sing their Zion songs, respond instead with a lament that is not really a song and ends with a bloodcurdling curse pronounced on their captors, who, fortunately, do not understand the Hebrew in which it is pronounced.

142: Allegedly David's song when he was hiding in a cave from Saul. He had extra time on his hands to work out all the chords.

143: I remember the days of old, G, back when you used to stand up for me. Bring back that lovin' feeling. Whoa, that lovin' . . .

144: Life is sweet when our kids grow to adulthood and no one's getting murdered in the town square. It's the little things, really.

145: In this ABC poem, the verse for the letter N was missing until Super Grover from *Sesame Stree*t found the Dead Sea Scrolls.

146: G gives food to the hungry, sets prisoners free, and cures the blind. Clearly, G is not a member of the Tea Party.

147: G fixes the number of stars and gives them names. So names like "Lambda Orionis" and "Eta Geminorum" are entirely his fault.

148: The following must report for praise duty: mountains, kings, sun, angels and waters. Sea monsters, drop and give G 20 pushups.

149: Let the people praise G with dancing! It's like that scene in *Footloose* when they use the Bible to show that G approves of the prom.

150: Praise for G's typical awesomeness. Praise with loud clanging cymbals. Praise that we're *finally* finishing the Psalter. Selah.

PROVERBS

Overview: What you'd get if *Rich Dad, Poor Dad* wed *The Seven Habits of Highly Effective People* and spawned call-in *Bible Talk Radio*.

1: Kids, if your gang says, "Hey! Let's go kill someone!" then Dame Wisdom says it's a subtle clue that you need new friends.

2: Kids, if you listen to your wise parents' advice, you'll know only good results. Well, except when they're 100% wrong.

3: Kids, G always disciplines those he loves. This hurts G more than it hurts you. Seriously. Spanking's kind of a compliment.

4: Kids, be sure to avoid the bread of wickedness and the wine of violence. They're still waiting for FDA approval.

5: Boys, don't have sex with loose foreign women. It never ends well. You'll thank us for all this advice later on, we promise. Much later.

The How-to Bible

A lot of people read the Bible hoping for concrete, practical tips for a successful life—the best ways to invest their money, choose a spouse, become better parents, or manage their time. For the most part, the Bible lets those people down because it generally can't be read as a self-help book. Instead it's a slapdash collection of stories, sayings, prophecies, letters, laws, and other miscellany, some of which is hard to relate to modern life.

But such concrete tips *are* found in the Book of Proverbs, which is chock-full of pragmatic advice for a happy, long, and prosperous life. What's ironic about that is that Proverbs is one of the most neglected and least utilized parts of the Bible, so people are strip mining other parts for how-to advice while ignoring this one book that contains said advice. "As a source of spiritual inspiration and guidance, [Proverbs] is almost lost to us," writes biblical scholar Ellen F. Davis. "We rarely hear from it in church, let alone at home. Probably few of us would be able to identify a verse from Proverbs, let alone recite one."

Maybe Proverbs is neglected because it's not organized the way contemporary readers would prefer: by topic. We want it arranged alphabetically by heading, with all of the marital wisdom in one section and career counseling in another. Instead we've got a mishmash of things—farming aphorisms and parenting strategies, thoughts on friendship and odes to wisdom—all dancing cheek to cheek.

Digging in to the book requires time and patience, but it's well worth the effort. Proverbs 14:23 tells us that there is profit to be found in hard work. Maybe some of that hard work could be directed toward understanding, and even memorizing, this book's wise sayings.

6: Wake up, lazybones! If an ant can get its own food and avoid hard times, there's no excuse for you. Get your butt out of bed.

7: Boys, Cautionary Tale #2 about dodgy sexy ladies, in case you missed chapter 5 because you were A) sleeping or B) out with a hooker.

8: Dame Wisdom on QVC: "Hear ye, hear ye! Those who seek me get love, honor, riches, knowledge, and this one-time-only set of Ginsu knives."

9: Dame Wisdom throws herself a quiet, elegant housewarming. Dame Folly down the street breaks out a six-pack and burps a little too loudly.

10: Here we get 20 chapters of wise sayings attributed to Solomon. Or his court secretaries. Or random people 500 years later. Whatever.

11: A lovely but dumb woman is like a gold ring in a pig's snout. A handsome but dumb man . . . Wait. Oddly, Proverbs doesn't mention him.

12: Be your own boss, tilling the land—not among the nouveau riche, eating chichi food and kvetching about the price of arugula.

13: James Dobson: "Spare the rod and spoil the child." Dr. Spock: "Never spank." Bible: "What they said." Now my head is exploding.

Five Money Rules
from the Book of Proverbs

What do these proverbs have to say about money and wealth?

1. Get rich slow. Proverbs takes a dim view of get-rich-quick schemes, in keeping with the book's general emphases on wise and industrious living. The authors of these proverbs don't really question the overall idea that having money is a nice comfort; Proverbs is not the place where you're going to find those "Go, sell all that you have" admonishments of that crazy Jesus guy in the New Testament. It just tells you to accumulate your nest egg slowly, "little by little" (Prov. 13:11, 28:20). Don't be greedy or hasty.

2. Give to the poor. While Proverbs doesn't highlight a particular percentage or amount that we're supposed to give to the poor, it's clear from start to finish that we're expected to be generous. When we oppress the poor, we insult God (Prov. 14:31, 17:5); when we ignore those who are suffering, God is likely to return the favor and not hear our prayers when we're in trouble ourselves (Prov. 21:13).

3. Don't be idle. Like, ever. Proverbs hammers home the point that work is vital to a fulfilling life. If ants can do it, so can you (Prov. 6:6–8)! Ideally, in the Bible's eyes, you'd be at work on your own land, raising your own food with your family or clan. Failing that, you can at least join a CSA and work diligently at whatever day job you've got. Hard work builds character, whereas idleness leads to destruction and watching reruns of *Jersey Shore* (Prov. 13:4, 12:24, 10:4).

4. Don't be too rich or too poor. Proverbs makes a strong case for the strength of the middle class: if you're too poor, you'll be prone to sins like theft and envy; if you're too rich, you'll cozy up to the things of this world and forget all about God (Prov. 30:8).

5. Get your priorities straight. Loving God and growing in wisdom are more important than money. Money is a fleeting thing that's of use for this brief life but no longer (Prov. 23:5, 27:23). The Bible says it's better to have a little money but be right with God than a lot of money you obtained unjustly (Prov. 16:8).

14: Those who oppress the poor insult G, and those who are kind to the poor are blessed. Why don't we live like we believe it?

15: A soft answer turns away wrath and a gentle tongue is the tree of life, but a snarky Twitter Bible only leads to trouble.

16: Pride goes before a fall. If you weren't so arrogant, you'd call 911 NOW as a prophylactic measure for when you fall.

17: Even fools look smart when they have the wisdom to close their mouths. We're all more intelligent when we shut the hell up.

18: On the difference between friend and frenemy: The friend's got your back. The frenemy's the one plunging a knife into it. Good to know.

19: When you're kind to the poor you actually lend money to G with interest! And T-bonds in the First Bank of G are rated AAA.

20: "The glory of youths is their strength, but the beauty of the aged is their gray hair." Take that, Miss Clairol.

21: Getting rich by means of a lying tongue is a snare of death. We're talking to you in the orange jumpsuit, Bernie Madoff.

22: Train children up in the way they should go, and when they are old they will not depart from it. Except when they do.

23: Red, red wine looks all sparkly in the chalice but comes back to bite your ass the next day. So stay off the sauce, OK?

Strong Woman

The "Proverbs 31 woman" has been used through the centuries both to praise women's strength and to keep them in their place, which many biblical interpreters have insisted is the home. But if you read the text more carefully, you can see it is a bit more complicated than that.

For starters, the word that is sometimes translated as "virtue" (as in, "The Woman of Virtue") actually means "strength." It's the same word that's used to describe military conquest (Num. 24:18) and physical prowess (2 Kings 24:16). According to Biblestudytools.com, most of the word's occurrences in the Old Testament (243 times total) appear in conjunction with mentions of armies, soldiers, military forces, valor, and wealth.

Also, the poem does more than *tell* us that she kicks ass; it shows us how by taking us through an A-to-Z litany of the many things this woman does each day. It's enough to make the Energizer Bunny feel defeated and lazy by comparison. Still, commenters through the years have demonstrated a remarkable ability to ignore what the text actually says and impose upon it their prejudices about women's roles in society and the family. Consider this so-awful-it's-almost-funny exegesis from *In Praise of Women*:

> If, as popular folklore has it, primitive man and his mate lived in a darkened cave, there is a good chance that on a snowy, cavebound winter day she announced that as soon as the weather warmed a little she intended to move the fire to another corner of the cave and suggested that as soon as he could get to moving around the countryside again he find some petrified wood for a table. And while he was at it, why not keep his eyes open for a beaver or two. She was sick of wearing these old rabbit skins!

One wonders what Bible these authors are reading, or perhaps what drugs they are smoking. In Proverbs, remember, it's the woman who "brings the food from far away" (v. 14) and supplies merchants (v. 24) with the cloth she has spun from her own wool (v. 13). And rather than cooling her jets in a cave, our heroine would instead have invested in prime real estate, since the text tells us she's plenty sharp enough to snap up a hot property when it comes on the market (v. 24). So let's do what the text orders us to: praise her for her achievements and the work of her hands (v. 31).

24: Don't rejoice when your enemies' lives turn to crap. Well, maybe just *one* little Snoopy dance of joy. But that's it.

25: Removing the wicked Congresspeople from D.C. is like taking dross out of silver. Seriously. I have a few I could nominate.

26: "Like a dog that returns to its vomit is a fool who reverts to his folly." Let's give the Bible props for memorable similes.

27: "As iron sharpens iron, so friends sharpen each other." Please note that this is only a metaphor. Do not carve your friends.

28: "Anyone who rebukes another will find more favor than those who flatter with empty words." Exercise caution when heeding this advice.

29: Hotheads, listen up: Only fools give full vent to their anger. So stop ranting, shock jocks. It makes you look awfully stupid.

30: Give me neither poverty nor riches, G. If I'm rich I'll deny you; if I'm poor I'll have to steal. Being middle class is a win-win.

31: Dawn to-do list: Buy real estate. Make winter coats. (Weave cloth first.) Make family look good. Be strong. Get Michelle Obama arms.

ECCLESIASTES

Overview: Grumpy pundit Qoheleth dishes on life, wisdom, vanity, and his neighbors. He's dead now, as he predicted. Ah, futility.

1: "Been there, done that. Same old, same old. I got nothin'. Life sucks and then you die. So eat, drink, and be merry while you still can!"

2: Q shocks all by saying that wisdom is overrated: The wise die, just like fools. Ironically, his book's now branded as wisdom literature.

3: To everything (turn, turn, turn) there is a season (turn, turn, turn). Except for orange plaid. There is absolutely NO season for that.

4: Q: "The dead are luckier than the living, but the really blessed are those who were never born at all." Um, thanks?

5: Q says rich people don't sleep well because of guilt over their extra wealth. FWIW, he'll totally contradict this in the next chapter.

6: Q: "What few days remain in your vain life are best spent enjoying wealth." Excuse us. The Bible has stepped out to Saks. Back in a mo.

7: Q says he's seen it all during his utterly meaningless life and warns: Don't be too good or too evil. It's complicated.

8: Q looks on as Mr. Wicked Evil Neighbor is buried with full honors and a sumptuous funeral. And . . . Q's back on the vanity train again.

9: "The dead are lost forever; they have no reward. Enjoy life while you can, since you'll be forgotten. Bottoms up, mate!"

10: The anti-Magnificat. Q tsk-tsks princes walking on foot while slaves ride on horseback. The rich deserve to rule, he says. Hmph.

11: Q says we don't know much about history. Don't know much theology. Don't know much about NOTHIN', so . . . don't worry. Be happy.

12: Of making many books there is no end, and most are a waste of trees. Of course, that didn't stop Q from writing a book of his very own.

SONG OF SOLOMON

Overview: The original sexting. Keeping youth group kids exposed to soft porn for approximately 2,300 years and counting. NC-17.

1: She says: "Kiss me on the mouth, you sexy babe, and take me with you RIGHT NOW. Our bed is verdant. Did I mention u r hot?"

2: "I'm faint with love. His left hand's under my head and his right arm is . . ." Wait. I need a cold shower. Taking a break.

3: Loverboy didn't come to bed tonight, so she combs the streets to hunt him down. Brings him home to meet Mom. Aaaaww.

4: What happened to pickup lines like "Your breasts are like twin gazelles"? I mean, really. Try it in a pub. I just dare you.

5: She tells her girlfriends that his lips are lilies dripping with myrrh and his arms are rods of gold. Keeps it fairly PG-13 though.

6: She may have overdone the praise of his ripped bod, because now the girlfriends want him too. Back off, ladies; he's already taken.

7: Loverboy says her rounded thighs are the beautiful work of a master hand. Where are men like this nowadays, I ask you?

8: Set me as a seal on your heart, for love is as strong as death. Now come to bed! We've had eight whole chapters of racy foreplay.

ISAIAH

Overview: Three different writers over 220+ years all call themselves Isaiah. Confusing much? Know for quiz: Pre-exile, exile, post-exile.

1: Fashion update: G changes "sin" color scheme from scarlet to pure white, a bold design choice. White is the new red.

2: Isa prophesies that G's vengeance is about to rain down on the proud pagans. Which means ALL y'all, Judah. Good times ahead.

3: All rise! Judge G has entered chambers. Sentences Judah to long exile in far-off penal colony. Judah cries foul: "Mistrial! Mistrial!"

4: G's particularly down on women in this chapter. Also the last chapter. OK, maybe the entire Old Testament. Sigh.

5: Woe to those who call evil good and good evil. Cause that makes no sense at all. They make dictionaries for people like that.

Three Different Isaiahs?

The Book of Isaiah is long—the longest prophetic book in the Bible—and sometimes confusing. Is it the Assyrians attacking us now, or the Babylonians? Who is king again? Which exile are we talking about here?

One theory about the book's complexity is that it was composed by multiple people in different historical situations. We'll never know definitively, but it can be helpful to think about Isaiah in three chunks.

First Isaiah (chapters 1-39): This is the prophet Isaiah who served during the reigns of several kings of Judah in the mid-eighth century BCE. Earlier, the Assyrians had invaded the northern kingdom of Israel, and it didn't take a prophet to guess that Judah might be next as Assyria extended its domination. So this longest section of Isaiah is taken up with the ominous threat of Assyria, and with Isaiah explaining why the people of Judah totally deserve to be overrun. As you can imagine, the people aren't best pleased to hear it.

Second Isaiah (chapters 40-55): This part of Isaiah seems to have been written later, probably during the Babylonian exile. Judah's people have been subdued and the city of Jerusalem laid waste, so you'd think this part of Isaiah would be full of woe and gnashing of teeth. (How does one gnash teeth, anyway?) However, this section is full of hope and comfort, as God promises to take care of his people once again if they'll only obey. If only.

Third Isaiah (chapters 56-66): Finally, this shortest section of Isaiah appears to have been written shortly after the second section. The exile is over and the people are home, but home isn't the bed of roses they had imagined. It's always something.

Note that the three-author theory is just that: a theory. Since scholars of the Bible argue even more vociferously than characters *in* the Bible, there's hardly universal agreement about any biblical interpretation, but it can be helpful context in following the basic plot.

6: Isa has a sentimental flashback about the moment he was first called to be a prophet and tell the people that they suck. Ah, happy day.

7: Isa: "See that young woman over there? By the time she bears a son, your lands will be laid waste by G's little friend Assyria."

8: Isa and his prophetess wife name their son Maher-shalal-hash-baz. He's going to have a heck of a time filling out forms when he grows up.

9: "For unto us a child is born & a son is given. The government shall be upon his shoulders." Let's hope he's been pumping iron to prepare.

10: G hires Assyria for the demolition stage of Israel's renovation. Unfortunately, most Israelites will not survive to see the Big Reveal.

11: After the destruction, the lion will lie with the lamb, and life will be rainbows and butterflies. But first, lots of folks have to die.

12: In the coming millennium, we'll all praise G, who was once really pissed at us but will finally be over it. Fingers crossed, anyway.

13: Back to reality. Before we get to the warm fuzzies of chapters 11 and 12, G still has to punish the wicked. Which, gulp, means us.

ISAIAH **157**

14: Someday, Israel, you'll taunt your conquerors like they're taunting you. At least it's something to dream about as you lose everything.

15: Moab's destroyed overnight. That would be bad enough, but now there's no place in the whole ancient world for us to go mountain biking.

16: If Moab were an orchard, its fruit trees would be dead. No more apple picking. No more pie . . . Wait, no PIE?! Now I'm scared.

17: An oracle against Damascus. Say, with predictions as dire as these, can we please hire a new prophet with a happier outlook?

18: G forecloses on the once-strong nation of Cush. Zillow says Israel's neighbors are contributing to declining real estate values.

19: If there's a silver lining to Assyria annihilating us, it's that G's an equal opportunity destroyer. Egypt's gonna bite it, too! ☺

20: G makes Isa go naked and barefoot for three years. Sometimes it's cold comfort to be the prophet. Wailing and teeth gnashing optional.

21: Babylon, Edom, and Arabia get their very own prophecies of death and mayhem! They had requested as much on their Amazon Wish Lists.

22: Jerusalem, just so you know, G's gonna seriously kick your ass with the coming exile. Don't say you weren't warned . . . AGAIN.

23: Last but not least on G's hit list is Tyre, whose great seaports will be closed for 70 years. Sorry, Carnival Cruises.

24: FYI, G plans to lay waste to the entire earth. Zombies may be involved. This has been a test of the Emergency Broadcast System.

25: Shortly after declaring global destruction, G perfects "No More Tears" formula and promises peace and love. Bipolar much?

26: Folks, go into your room and lock the door. Please hide there until G's wrath subsides and he stops playing World of Warcraft.

27: "On that day G will come with his great and terrible sword" to slay our dragons. G, feel free to do that anytime. Or send Saint George.

28: The prophet commences a list of "Six Woes," starting with Samaria and Judah. Weirdly, they're not pleased to receive top billing.

29: G: "Because you pay me lip service while your hearts are far from me, I'll give your Wii to the Assyrians and put you in a long timeout."

30: G charges Isa to write the truth and put it in a book. If it's in a book, then all the obstinate people will listen. That always works.

31: Woe to you who rely on Egypt. Despite how things may seem right now, G's actually stronger than Pharaoh. Recall that whole Exodus thing?

32: G predicts that in the future we'll have fair governments and leaders who show good judgment. Most far-fetched prophecy in the Bible.

33: G tells enemies that when they stop destroying, they'll be destroyed themselves. This is not fabulous motivation for them to change.

Have a Little Faith

More ink has been spilled on the famous prophecy "behold, a virgin shall conceive" than perhaps any other in Isaiah, in part because of many Christians' determination to make the text fit with the later birth of Christ. Despite the fact that the word "virgin" in the passage is more accurately translated "young woman," and despite the fact that there's plenty of historical context to explain what the prophecy meant to Isaiah, King Ahaz, and the people of Jerusalem in the eighth century, many people have persisted in lifting that verse out of the whole of Isaiah and giving it a life of its own. (Thank you, Handel!)

But the prophecy's original context is every bit as inspiring. When it came up in conversation, Isaiah was trying desperately to convince King Ahaz about the seriousness of the Assyrian threat. At the time, Ahaz was worrying incessantly about two minor threats while ignoring Assyria, which Isaiah endeavored to convince him was the larger menace. To hammer home the point and to set an example via "Take Your Kids to Work Day," the prophet had even brought along his own son to the meeting. Prophets were not known for subtlety in naming their children—just wait until we get to Hosea!—and his son's name was as significant as it was awkward: it meant "a remnant shall return."

That a remnant would return suggested that there would be a departure in the first place. Which was not news the king especially wanted to hear at this juncture.

Isaiah was trying to encourage Ahaz to have faith: faith that God was still in charge, and that the covenant was still in force. But Ahaz refused to take a chance on trusting the God of Israel because his own efforts and devices seemed so much more reliable. In the end, perhaps the best contemporary application of this prophecy is that through the ages, people have always struggled with trusting God. They often choose to lean on their own understanding—to their later regret.

34: G will have a day of revenge, a year of vindication, and destruction that lasts for generations. It seems he's getting on a roll.

35: Post-exile vision: The blind will see, the lame will leap, and you'll all get a nice big lollipop. Like after a shot at the doctor's. OK?

36: The Assyrian king is banging on the gates! The northern kingdom has fallen and things look very bad for Judah too. A real nail-biter.

37: King Hez prays about what to pack for the Assyrian exile, but . . . wait! G says Jerusalem can still be saved. (OMG! Unexpected.)

38: G gives King Hez 15 more years and saves the city. Close call + Hollywood ending = ready-made sequel: *The Exile Returns*.

39: First Isaiah ends. It's 200 years later when we land in Second Isaiah, which is more tender, we promise. It's shorter, with less death.

40: Comfort ye my people. Returnees will get heating pads, hot cocoa, and backrubs from the same God who sent them to Timbuktu.

41: "Don't fear, for I am with you." It's nice to hear that G came along for the exile, even if he does call us worms in verse 14. (Worms?!)

42: Breaking news! G's chosen servant will bring justice, become a light to the nations, and #occupywallstreet.

On Eagles' Wings

. . . but those who wait for the Lord shall renew their strength,
they shall mount up with wings like eagles,
they shall run and not be weary,
they shall walk and not faint. (Isa. 40:31)

Who doesn't want to be an eagle, soaring high above it all? And who wouldn't love this passage's promise that we shall mount up with eagles' wings?

But something important happens to our view of ourselves and our God if the Hebrew word we've always translated as "eagles" turns out to mean "vultures" instead. As Debbie Blue reflects in *Consider the Birds*,

> Isaiah may actually have meant to say that those who wait shall mount up with wings like vultures—not eagles. Faith is more like circling than seizing. It is being lifted by thermals more than flying by the power of our individual wings.
>
> We've formed some ideas of God and faith with the eagle in mind. The vulture God might give us a different perspective. Whether we are reading scripture as first-century Jews or twenty-first-century Christians, the Word seems to have the sort of life that continually startles. People may have been reading it carefully for thousands of years but this doesn't mean something new might not walk out of it. Isaiah points to a messiah (a savior) who "possessed no splendid form for us to see, no desirable appearance." In the gospels we encounter a God who comes and dies. If we hope to hear the word of God in the Scripture, it might be good to listen as though we don't already always know what it's going to say.

43: G says not to remember the past. Get amnesia already, or a lobotomy. Fuhgeddaboudit. G's on to a new thing, starting now.

44: G: "I'm the first and the last. Besides me there is no god. So stop trying to make idols for yourselves out of Lincoln Logs, OK?"

45: Cyrus, the Persian king, is G's anointed. He sends Israel home from exile so he can pursue a secret life as Hannah Montana.

46: G: "Remember the former things of old." Which suggests that G's forgotten what he said in chapter 43. Do deities have senior moments?

47: Remember how Second Isa lays off the smiting? That doesn't apply to Babylon, which gets, well, smitten. And not in a lovey-dovey way.

48: G gives a "Dad speech": You'd have gotten the chocolate factory if only you'd obeyed. It's as successful as such sermons usually are.

49: "Can a woman forget her nursing child?" G has compassion on us even though we cause mastitis. 1-800-MOM-LOVE.

50: The prophet kvetches that he's followed G faithfully but no one ever listens to him. Given Israel's record, he's surprised by this?

51: "The earth will wear out like a garment, and all the living will die like gnats." I feel uplifted somehow. And you?

It Sucks to Be the Prophet

It was very, very hard to be a prophet in the times of the Hebrew Bible/Old Testament. Sure, there were high points, like Elijah routing the priests of Baal or Isaiah glimpsing the Lord. But most days, a career in prophecy was no picnic. Here are some low moments for a few prophets of the Bible:

Isaiah: Ordered to go naked and barefoot for three years (Isa. 20). Rejected by the people.

Jeremiah: Imprisoned (Jer. 18) and thrown down a well (Jer. 37–38). Rejected by the people.

Ezekiel: Told to lie on his side and eat only bread and water for over a year (Ezek. 4). Required to cut his hair into thirds (Ezek. 5). Rejected by the people.

Hosea: Commanded to marry a prostitute and give his children psychologically damaging names (Hos. 1–2). Rejected by the people.

Jonah: Swallowed by a giant fish after being dispatched to preach the gospel to Nineveh (Jon. 1–2). *Not* rejected by the people, which is why this story is probably fiction.

52: "How lovely on the mountains are the feet of him who brings good news." P.S. The messenger got his stylin' boots from Zappos.

53: The suffering servant will be despised, rejected, then wounded for our transgressions. It's a plum job. Any volunteers?

54: After the exile, your family will expand even faster than the Duggars. Multiple blessings ahead. Bottom line: Supersize your tent.

55: G says his thoughts are not our thoughts. No kidding. I, for example, wouldn't have murdered the Midianites in Numbers 31. Just saying.

56: Attention, all eunuchs! You're now officially part of Israel. You won't be cut off even if your, um, you-know-what was cut off.

57: We're in Third Isaiah now and it's about 20 years later. Jews have postexilic homecoming parade. What, no game or bonfire?

58: The people are ticked that G hasn't given them a gold star yet for fasting. An annoyed G sends them to bed without any dinner.

59: "We wait for justice, but there is none." It's Gotham City without Batman down here, people. We need a Dark Knight to kick some A!

60: Arise, shine! Your light has come. It's no use hitting the snooze button, loser. Isn't G's divine glory worth getting out of bed for?

61: The spirit of G has sent me to preach good news to the oppressed, release the prisoners, etc. Well, someone has to do it.

62: Israel, you will now be called My-Delight-Is-in-Her. G suggests you reserve that domain name right away before he changes his mind.

63: "Why, O Lord, do YOU make US stray from your ways?" Mistakes were made, but not by us. That's our story and we're sticking to it. Yep.

64: O that you would tear open the heavens and come down! And that you would stop being so mad at us. If it's not too much to ask.

65: You know how in *Battlestar Galactica* they finally find Earth but it's a toxic wasteland? Returning to Jerusalem after exile is like that.

66: Isaiah ends on a high note as we eagerly anticipate the death and destruction of our enemies. *Such* good times ahead.

JEREMIAH

Overview: FYI, this is the prophet who invented the "jeremiad," or long lament of doom. So don't expect lots of jolly, inspiring pep talks.

1: G to Jer: "Attack you they will. Overcome you they can't. Ready are you? For 800 years have I trained prophets. Hmm? Hmm."

2: G recalls when Isr was like a bride who had the hots for him alone, but now she's shamelessly horny. G files for The Big D. ☹

3: Gotta get a get! Isr gains an official divorce; continues sowing wild oats as swinging single. Texts Baal to arrange hookup.

4: G lays out the conditions for what Isr has to do if she ever wants to reunite. G's therapist is very proud G was so firm and clear.

5: G vents aloud about his ex-wife Isr, threatening to withhold alimony and even hire a hit man. Clearly, he's not over her yet.

6: Jer's tired of preaching doom, but G tells him to suck it up and pour on the brimstone: "Be Jonathan Edwards. On steroids."

7: G's moved out of the temple and won't come home until ex-wife Isr stops doing the nasty with Baal. G lives off microwave burritos.

8: This is where Jer could say "I told you so," but he's genuinely sad that all the people are going to die. He only *sounds* mean.

9: Jer wishes his eyes were a fountain of tears so he could weep day and night for Jerusalem. Get the poor man some Zoloft.

10: Chasten us, G, but not just now when you're so obviously ticked. Anger management specialists advise a 24-hour cooling off period. OK?

11: G begins a new policy of wearing noise-canceling headphones every time Judah prays. "What's that, Judah? I can't HEAR you . . ."

12: Jer grumbles to G about injustice, but G sees his complaint and raises him a lament. *Everyone* is unhappy in this book.

13: Jer's sexy new loincloth from Victoria's Secret becomes a sign of Judah's ruin when G trashes it. This chapter is one for the Weird File.

The Jeremiad

Here's a cool word inspired by the Bible: jeremiad. A jeremiad is any long, lamenting speech or piece of writing that bemoans the state of society. The Puritans elevated it to an art form. True to the spirit of the prophet Jeremiah, for whom it is named, any jeremiad worth its salt is going to conclude with some kind of dire prophecy about the coming demise of society or the world as we know it.

To practice being more biblically attuned at home, try giving jeremiads to/at/in the general direction of your children. Here is a template:

> For lo, these children's hearts have become corrupted, and they have wandered far from me. How far they have wandered, these children I raised from mere zygotes! For they were nothing, and I gave them everything; they were as dust, and I provided them with Gerber and Go-Gurt and every good food that is upon the earth. And now I will take from them their comforts, their stuffed bears and blankies, and I will make them sit in the time-out chair for an age. In bitterness and sorrow shall they pack their own lunches and drive themselves to preschool; thus saith the Lord.

Modern parents may look at the foregoing lament and worry that if they were ever to voice such disappointment, their children would be scarred for life. There is no need to fret about this. In all of history, no people who were ever the subject of a jeremiad ever actually listened to what was being said. It is purely a rhetorical exercise. Proceed.

14: G tells Jer to stop praying for the people because G's not going to listen anyway. It's good to be up front and transparent about that.

15: Jer: "Woe is me!" It should actually be "Woe is I," but grammar's the least of Jer's issues just now, so we'll let it slide.

16: G: "Lucky you, Jer. You get to stay celibate! I'll be butchering the nation's wives and kids soon, so I'm doing you a favor. Really."

17: Jer: "Behind Door #1 is the Way of Blessing; behind Door #2 is the Way of Death." You'd think it would be obvious, but not so much.

18: So it turns out that the people don't really want to hear that the exile was their fault. They imprison Jeremiah. Go figure.

19: G: "Jer, go publish the 'I'm the potter, you're the clay' metaphor. Tell them I'll crush them like china!" Oddly, this doesn't go viral.

20: Jer has to spend the night in the stocks and becomes a literal laughingstock. Sues career counselor G for nudging him toward prophecy.

21: Judah, if you're hoping G will mount a miraculous defense when Babylon comes knocking, think again. G's on their side now.

22: Jer charges the king with making Judah's own citizens be his slaves. With SOB kings like these, who needs enemies like Babylon?

23: Jer utters five statements denouncing false prophets. Which, in case you were wondering, does not include him. Just so we're clear.

24: "Those who stay in Jerusalem post-conquest are like rotten figs, unfit for eating." Wait a minute. G wants to EAT us now?!

25: Unknown editor enters the text to give Jer's prophecies some much-needed historical context. It's about freakin' time. Up with editors.

26: Jer receives a Mafia death threat for being such a party pooper. Jer: "Go ahead. Make. My. Day." Freaked-out mob backs off.

27: Bible politics Q: "Should we rebel against Babylon?" A: "Not if you value your city, temple, and necks." Hindsight's a bitch.

28: Jer and Hananiah in death match! But don't bet on Han here. No one ever profits from betting against a prophet.

29: Jer to exiles: "Marry locals and enjoy the hanging gardens in Babylon, cause you'll be there 70 years!" This advice is not popular.

30: Amidst death, war, and exile, G sends Israel and Judah a Hallmark card. The sentimental kind. NOW G cares enough to send the very best?

31: Deuteronomy 24 forbade remarriage to a two-timing wife, but G wrote the law and G can darn well break it. Reunited and it feels so good . . .

I Know the Plans I Have for You

If you do a Google image search for Jeremiah 29:11, you will come up with countless inspirational items depicting this verse on posters, t-shirts, mugs, and greeting cards:

> For surely I know the plans I have for you, says the Lord, plans for your welfare and not for harm, to give you a future with hope.

Isn't that a lovely message? I'm not even being sarcastic here; it's a beautiful verse that demonstrates God's care and provision in some future time.

Some very far future time. And that's where the posters and greeting cards take this verse completely out of the context of the Book of Jeremiah. This prophecy is not intended for an individual, but for an entire nation that is being uprooted and driven from its homeland. Moreover, the promise is delivered in the context of God telling these people that he is about to abandon them for the next seventy years. Seventy years! God advises them that during this time they should let their children marry the children of Babylon (Jer. 29:6). This must have been shocking advice to Judeans who had been told for centuries by this very same God not to intermarry—no way, no how. God wants them to be good citizens of Babylon while they're stuck there. They are to seek its welfare—getting involved in City Council, planting gardens, building houses (Jer. 29:5, 7).

And during those seventy years, God says, he will not attend to his people. Only when their long exile is concluded will he start hearing their prayers again when they call (Jer. 29:12); until then he will observe strict radio silence. It is in the context of this harsh sentence that the "I know the plans I have for you" verse comes into play.

So if you insist on applying this verse to your own difficulties—and yeah, I do it too—do so with some humility. God is playing a long game in Jeremiah. Many of the people he sent into exile didn't survive to see the end of their captivity, proving that God's timeline is often different than our own.

32: Insider trading: G tells Barouk who tells Maria who tells Zedekiah who tells Haroum that the real estate market will rebound.

33: G: "Your houses won't be able to *hold* all the bodies of the folks I'm going to kill before I decide I like you again, Judah."

34: G tells Judah, "Don't enslave your fellow Hebrews!" They agree, then change their minds. It's just so handy to have slaves.

35: G uses the example of the obedient Rekabites to shame Judah. That's like your parents saying, "Why can't you be more like your brother?"

36: G has Jer record all the nasty predictions and read them to the king, who just feeds the scroll pieces into the fire. DENIAL.

37: Orange is the new black. King Zed imprisons Jer for desertion, which is ironic since the king always wanted Jer to go away.

38: Jeremiah's tossed into a well of despair. He's already been there for a long time metaphorically, but now it's an actual well.

39: Siege! Invaders put the king's eyes out, but not before he sees his sons killed. Just another happy Sunday School lesson.

40: Jer declines a guard's offer to be his sugar daddy. Why is a Babylonian the first person to be nice to Jer in this entire book?

41: It's been just five minutes since the Babylonians took over and we already have our first coup. Who says the Bible's not fast-paced?

42: Let's ask G for advice: "Do we remain in Judah or abscond to Egypt?" G: "Stay!" So of course we'll go. Glad we had this little chat, G.

43: Jer's kidnapped and taken to Egypt. Everyone *talks* about living in BFE, but Jer actually does now. It's basically awful.

44: Although Jer's in Egypt now and the exile already happened, he's still preaching doom and mayhem. Old habits die hard: "Repent!"

45: We interrupt Jer's story for quick reassurance to the scribe Barach, who has major depression but whose life will be spared.

46: G tells Judah that he will not *completely* destroy her. There might be a tree left standing. If he's in a decent mood.

47: G says the day has come to annihilate all Philistines. This is fair punishment for never learning to appreciate opera.

48: During his killing spree, G will destroy the nation of Moab and silence its village called Madmen. He's that angry at Don Draper.

49: G says Ammon, Edom, Damascus, Kedar, Hazor, and Elam will all die painful deaths. Don't you feel better, Judah? It's not just you.

50: Babylon, you might want to stop gloating about being conquerors. G says your comeuppance is, um, coming up. And soon.

51: G: "Babylon's doomed. Run for your lives, Judah! Sure, I was the one who sent you there, but let's not quibble about the past."

52: The final chapter of Jeremiah recounts how Babylon plundered all the best goodies from G's temple. Those damn interlopers.

LAMENTATIONS

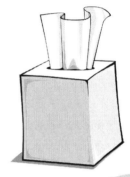

Overview: With a name like Lamentations, you *know* it has to be fun. If fun for you is an A-to-Z report of exile, death, and no HDTV.

1: Exile ABCs: Abandoned, betrayed, cracked, dead, exiled, forgotten, gloomy, hated, isolated, jagged. Kaput. (Please send chocolate.)

2: Exile ABCs continued: Loss, mourning, nothingness, obsolescence, priestlessness, rejection, slavery. Are we having fun yet?

3: Exile ABCs finale: Terror, uncertainty, violence, wrath, xenophobia. Yikes! Zero left of what we used to have.

4: More of the same. This chapter is still part of the alphabetical exile poem, but I got too sad. I also ran out of letters. #LAMEmentations

5: Lamentations ends with Judah bleating that G has turned its dancing into mourning. They liked the Psalm 30 version of that much better.

 LAMENTATIONS **179**

EZEKIEL

Overview: Anyone under age 30 isn't supposed to read this book. There's some CRAZY crap in here. (But psst, you can use a fake ID.)

1: July 31, 593 BCE: Zeke's just chilling out by the river when he has the Bible's trippiest vision to date. And that's saying something.

2: G gives Zeke a prophecy so long it fills two sides of a scroll. Then Zeke has to eat it—every bite, or he won't get dessert.

3: Though the scroll's packed with dire, gloomy words, it tastes sweet to Zeke. Jessica Seinfeld would call it deceptively delicious.

4: G has Zeke build a Lego model of Jerusalem, then put it under siege and starve out the Lego people—the Bible's idea of a fun play date.

5: Zeke cuts his own hair in thirds. 1/3 is burned, 1/3 is sliced up, and 1/3 is scattered. Object lesson: "This is Jerusalem!" Ah. Not good.

Ezekiel Bread

The Bible doesn't contain many recipes; it's more concerned with telling people what not to eat than prescribing specific things they should. However, it does have one interesting scene in which God instructs the prophet Ezekiel to make a particular kind of bread:

> And you, take wheat and barley, beans and lentils, millet and spelt; put them into one vessel, and make bread for yourself. During the number of days that you lie on your side, three hundred ninety days, you shall eat it. The food that you eat shall be twenty shekels a day by weight; at fixed times you shall eat it. . . . You shall eat it as a barley-cake, baking it in their sight on human dung. (Ezek. 4:9, 12)

In the context of the Book of Ezekiel, the recipe is not put forward as a delightful whole-grain alternative to processed foods, but as a sign of God's coming punishment of the people. The message was something like, "If you all don't repent, then this is the kind of survivalist garbage you will be reduced to eating during the coming siege!"

But that hasn't stopped some modern people from treating this recipe as a sign of the healthy, nutritious fare God would have for us today. The Food for Life company produces and markets several versions of Ezekiel 4:9 bread, including variations with sesame, flax, and—I kid you not—cinnamon-raisin.

Although the company has mostly adhered to the letter of the law in terms of ingredients, one hopes that its method of preparation has been modernized from Ezekiel's, who was instructed to bake his bread in human excrement. When Ezekiel protested about the unhygienic source material of his meals, God relented a little, allowing him to use cow dung instead (Ezek. 4:15). So when Food for Life's website encourages consumers to "try [the bread] served warm to release its exceptionally rich nutty flavor," I just don't think so.

6: When the corpses of the slain are scattered and the cities are laid waste, you'll know YHWH is Lord. And you'll, um, love him . . . ?

7: Since the people didn't pay attention to either the Lego model or the hair analogy, G turns to poetry here. That'll teach 'em for sure.

8: The Ghost of Exile Future gives another scary vision—this one of Abomination HQ, the temple. It's the Unholy of Unholies. Uh oh.

9: G commands us to go and slaughter unbelievers, even little kids. (P.S. Sometimes it's best to entirely ignore the Bible. Just a thought.)

10: G's glory departs from the city. That's like in *Star Trek* when the shields go down and they're vulnerable to Klingon attack. A bad sign.

11: G moves out of the Jerusalem temple but fails to file a change of address card with the post office. Present whereabouts unknown.

12: People convince themselves that Zeke's visions are for some distant future time in a galaxy far, far away. They feel much better now.

13: G rails against false prophets whose message is too upbeat. "What part of 'total annihilation' did you not understand, liars?"

The F Word Is in the Bible?!

As another entry in my "I never knew *that* was in the Bible" list, Ezekiel uses the equivalent of the F word in chapter 16. In fact, this whole chapter should be labeled as inappropriate for children, and possibly for everyone.

Here the prophet outlines all the many reasons that Israel is a whore. The *Eerdmans Commentary on the Bible* summarizes the chapter in this way:

> Ezekiel writes to shock and to shake, and reaches his most shocking so far here in this epic portrayal of the harrowing life story of Ms. Jerusalem. . . It is the prophetic equivalent to a four-hour movie blockbuster with repeated scenes of sexual violence and violence on children, which no one under 18 is allowed to see. It became another passage in Ezekiel which rabbinic leadership hesitated to have read in worship.

It's not just that Ezekiel uses the most damning language he can think of to condemn Israel's faithlessness and spiritual adultery. It's that the sexual metaphors are, shall we say, explicit: in one passage, Israel melts down the gold and silver that God has given her, only to make idols of male genitalia for purposes of twerking; in another, she is said to spread her legs for every passerby. (The NRSV relates this more gently as Israel "offering" herself.) And wait until we get to chapter 23, in which Israel is said to lust after male gods who have genitals the size of donkeys'.

I think I'll stop there. You get the idea.

14: G: "Even if the righteous Noah and Job were in Jerusalem, I'd still destroy it." As if he'd spared Job the first time. Puh-leeze.

15: Short, pithy chapter with our 426th allegory of Jerusalem's impending total destruction. 425 examples weren't nearly enough.

16: G uses the F word! Right there in the Bible! He's so sick of us effing around with other gods that he cusses like a sailor. Whoa.

17: A once-upon-a-time fable with eagles as characters. G tried to interest a children's publisher, but the ending was too dark.

18: G scraps the Exodus 20:5 "sins upon the fourth generation" schtick. Plan B: We're to blame for our sins but not our parents'. Thx!

19: The kingdom of Judah is like a lioness with two wayward cubs named Simba who disappeared from Pride Rock in shame. Wait, wrong story.

20: Remember: Only you can prevent forest fires in the Negeb. G's gonna turn arsonist on you if y'all don't change your wicked ways.

21: G says that his sword, Babylon, is so potent you're going to wet yourself with fear. Is this the first mention of urine in the Bible?

22: G wants us to stand in the gap: not just for our buddies, but for sinners. G continues raising the bar. I can't keep up.

23: G tells a story of two prostitutes (hint: one is Jerusalem) whose lovers had genitals like donkeys. Man, Ezekiel is one earthy book.

24: G deliberately burns dinner in a failed cooking experiment. That would be fine, except that the pot in this story is YOU. Oh.

25: This is the passage that Samuel L. Jackson quotes in *Pulp Fiction* just before each kill. Please don't try this exegesis at home.

26: The sea city of Tyre is going DOWN: "I will bring you to a horrible end and you will be no more." Iceberg, right ahead!

27: Zeke offers a lament for the Tyre-tanic after it's swallowed into the sea. And people said it was unsinkable. As if.

Don't Trust Anyone Under Thirty

Ezekiel is believed to have been thirty years old when God called him to be a prophet. And that was a good thing, because as we've seen, some of the contents of his prophetic revelations weren't exactly rated PG. But there were also other difficulties with understanding this disturbing book, so much so that some early rabbis restricted its study to those over the age of thirty and even limited the class size of groups that wanted to read it privately.

Bottom line: You might want to skip over this book for your child's bar or bat mitzvah *haftorah*. Just a suggestion.

28: G's still not done with the laundry list of everything Tyre's people did wrong. They'd feel guilty, except they're already dead.

29: Egypt's next, but instead of drowning the land, G makes it a desert waste. A new mode of death! G's nothing if not creative.

30: G breaks both of Pharaoh's arms, then finishes him off with a Babylonian hit man. Wins career-making role as Tony Soprano.

31: G sees that his metaphors of sea disasters and parched earth are falling on deaf ears, so he turns to "trees felled in forest." Yawn.

32: Phar's condemned to the realm of the dead to hang out with all the uncircumcised folks G annihilated. They pass the time playing cards.

33: G makes Zeke "watchman for Israel" and warns that if he falls asleep on the job he'll be slain on the spot. This is why we need unions.

34: G runs for Shepherd! Makes lavish campaign promises of peace and prosperity. Harsh smear campaign against his rivals, though.

35: Although we already had a nasty oracle against Edom, here's another. Yes, the Edomites are *that* bad. Wait till we get to Obadiah.

36: G says Israel used to be as unclean as a woman with her period. Which, if you haven't guessed, is not a compliment.

37: Dem bones, dem bones, dem dry bones. Now hear the word of the Lord: Toe bone connected to the foot bone. Foot bone . . .

38: Zeke glimpses great battle at the end of time: Gog will go to war against Israel and lose. I'm all . . . agog. Sorry, I couldn't resist.

39: G announces the end of the exile. No more suffering! Well, a little less, at any rate. Y'all come on home from Babylon now, y'hear?

40: Thus begin the benign, happier last chapters of Ezekiel. It's good to end on a high note after all that death and genocide.

41: Zeke gets VIP virtual tour of the temple, but next to his visions of UFOs etc., this one's pretty dull. Mostly an architecture lecture.

42: Virtual tour resumes with a backstage pass to the hermetically sealed Holy of Holies. It's way cooler than the one in the first temple.

43: Breaking news! G might be returning to his temple after all. Keep those east doors open and run the vacuum, just in case.

44: Rituals of purity for the temple's priests. Takeaway point: Just be relieved you're not one of them. OCD teetotalers all.

45: Zeke's brave new imagined world continues by mandating total ritual purity. This society is *not* going to sin again, no sir.

46: A crash course in temple etiquette: Never enter and leave by the same door. Don't ask why. It's just rude.

47: G's spirit returns to the temple, but in a rush of water. We're glad you're back, G, but can you call a plumber for us?

48: No more violence, oppression, or exile! The people are righteous again, so Zeke's unemployed. He seems kinda glad about it though.

Attention: God Is in the Building

The final chapters of Ezekiel are taken up with the hope, solidifying in Ezekiel's prophetic imaginings, of God returning to the Jerusalem temple. Now, God's presence or absence from the temple was a Very Big Deal in the Hebrew Bible/Old Testament. Since the time of Solomon, the people of Jerusalem had put total stock in the promise that God would never abandon his house. Shortly after the temple's dedication centuries before, God had told Solomon, "I have consecrated this house that you have built, and put my name there forever; my eyes and my heart will be there for all time" (1 Kings 9:3).

But the people had a remarkable ability to cling to the promise of God as a permanent protector while ignoring the inconvenient conditions that insisted that God's protection was contingent upon their righteousness. We human beings tend to hear only what we want to hear, and the people of Jerusalem refused to countenance any notion that God might someday abandon his chosen abode.

But abandon it he did, allowing the Babylonians to destroy the temple and the city, and crushing the people's hopes. Most of the freaky-scary parts of the first two-thirds of the Book of Ezekiel spell out—often in graphic detail—the reasons why such divine desertion was entirely the fault of the people. Yet there are hopeful moments, such as when Ezekiel commands a field of dead bones to live or prophesies that the "sticks" of Ephraim/Israel and Judah will once again become one stick, a single reunited nation as in the days of old (Ezek. 37).

The restoration of the temple was an important component of that hopeful vision of national glory, and the final chapters of Ezekiel recount what the future temple would someday be like. The rushing water of chapter 47 is a metaphor for the fierce, overabundant Spirit that will return in full force to that temple-to-be. This message must only have brought hope and wonder to the exiled people, despite their worries about whether they would be able to afford to pay the plumber.

DANIEL

Overview: Righteous Jew stands up, stands up for kosher in the Babylonian court. Say, what's that smell? Is something burning?

1: Jews Hananiah, Mishael, and Azariah are forced to use imperial names of Shadrach, Meshach, and Abednego. Like those are simpler.

2: Dr. Dan Freud, Chief Dream Interpreter. *Wunderkinder* Dan & Co move up corporate ladder to high positions in Neb's court.

3: Refusal to bow down before idol lands Shad and friends in fiery furnace. But who's this fourth person saving them? An angel? God? Batman?

4: Dan says King Neb's latest dream means Neb will be driven from society, start grazing like a cow, and need a manicurist in the worst way.

5: New king has Dan decode strange writing. Dan: "The saying 'read the writing on the wall' will last forever. But your reign? Two hours."

DANIEL 191

6: Dan's now on his third king: Darius. But he arrests Dan for praying three times a day. Because that is very wrong. Lion jaws are looming.

7: Dan's rescued from the lion's den, but is plagued with PTSD vision of four beasts, judgment, etc. He shuts down and won't discuss it.

8: Dan's weird visions make no sense to him until the Angel Gabriel appears to interpret. So when will Gabe explain the whole Bible to US?

9: Dan confesses Israel's sin and prays for forgiveness. Then Gabe gives a full-on apocalyptic lecture that's about as clear as mud.

10: Dan avoids meat, wine, and lotion for three weeks, then receives new vision. Moral: If you want a revelation, shun Jergens at all costs.

11: Prophecy 101. The king of the South will attack the king of the North. It'll be like the Civil War, only in Aramaic! Won't that be fun.

12: Daniel's big finish is an apocalyptic vision of the end of days. It's always good to close with a little drama.

HOSEA

Overview: G orders prophet Hosea to marry a whore. This is a recipe for disaster, especially since she refused her early retirement package.

1: Quick allegory tips. So, the hooker/wife is supposed to be you. G's played by the prophet, even though he's the one named "Ho." Got it?

2: Ho's kids are called "Not Pitied" and "Not My People." It's so odd that these aren't found in today's Bible baby name books.

3: G still loves Israel, but her whoring people are turning to other gods and devouring raisin cakes. Apparently raisin cakes are eeee-vil.

4: In the criminal justice system are two separate and unequal groups: the people who commit crimes and the DA God with 100% convictions.

5: G wrings his hands, wondering what to do with rebelling teens Israel and Judah. It's time for some tough love. Every parent can relate.

6: G: "It used to be thieves who'd murder innocent people at the roadside. Now it's my own priests. Can you believe it? These kids today!"

7: Israel: "Dear gods of Egypt and Assyria, give us grain and other good stuff! We ♥ you. SWAK." G: "Hey, what am I, chopped liver?"

8: G writes directions for "How Not to Sin" in triplicate and circulates leaflets, but Israel develops Sudden Illiteracy Syndrome.

9: Spoilsport Hosea crashes Sukkoth festival to warn Israel of its coming danger, but they're busy with wine and song. Get him, bouncers!

10: G says Israel's fancy altars don't amount to a hill of beans cause he's not feeling the love. Pines for the good old days.

11: G reminisces about when baby Israel learned to walk and eat solids. They turn evil so fast, don't they? It's hard being a dad.

12: G decides to send rebelling teen Israel on Outward Bound experience for at-risk youth. Hmm, that Assyria program looks good . . .

13: G: "Who fed you in the wilderness, huh? Who's your daddy? Well, the hand that cared for you can also bring you DOWN."

14: G welcomes a duly chastened Israel back from Assyrian time-out and forgives all. Quick! Kill the fatted calf before this honeymoon ends.

Twelve Angry Men

Hosea begins the section of the Bible called the "Twelve Minor Prophets," which is basically all the little guys who didn't score full-scale books like Isaiah, Jeremiah, and Ezekiel did. The longest books in the Minor Prophets are Hosea and Zechariah, with fourteen chapters apiece; the shortest is Obadiah, which has just one. (Don't worry. It gets its point across with admirable concision.)

Most of the books contain some autobiographical material as well as speeches by the prophets, who harangue the people for various sins and give dreadful warnings about the calamities that will occur if they don't clean up their act. There are some exceptions, like Jonah, which is a third-person story without any autobiographical material. That stuff was in Jonah's first draft, but a fish ate his homework.

The Minor Prophets spanned several centuries and geographic locations. Amos and Hosea lived in the eighth century and were trying to convince folks in the north that Assyria was about to gobble them up if they didn't change their ways; Haggai and Zechariah lived much later, in the south, during the general time of Ezra and Nehemiah. Their main concerns were to speed up the rebuilding of the Jerusalem temple and to convince the people not to backslide into the wickedness that got them exiled in the first place.

JOEL

Overview: Attention: The day of YHWH is at hand. The day of YHWH is at hand. This has been a public service announcement.

1: An army of locusts descends and gobbles everything in sight. Is the day of YHWH really near? Best to fast and pray, young grasshoppa.

2: G will pour out his spirit for dreams and visions, even on women, kids, old folks, and slaves. It's a Universal Prophecy Care Program.

3: Prophet Joel changes tune: "Everything's great! You're doing so well! Don't change a thing!" Nah, just kidding. He still thinks you suck.

AMOS

Overview: Reverse carpetbagging. Prophet Amos travels from South to North to tell folks how things should be done. But they never listen.

1: G: "For your neighbors' three—wait, four!—war crimes, I won't relent. They're as violent as that Mortal Kombat game. I *hate* that game."

2: G: "Judah, I heard you laughing while I punished your neighbors. But I've saved the best judgment for last, jerk. It's your turn."

3: The people react to Amos's censure with a classic "Who the hell are you?" defense. Shooting the messenger: old but remarkably effective.

4: Amos calls the local women "cows of Bashan" because they do their nails while the poor go hungry. Way to woo the ladies, Casanova.

Israel

Keeping the Sabbath ... F
Caring for the Poor ... F
Avoiding Incest ... F
Loving Worship ... F
Learning from the Past ... F
Staying Humble ... F

Please come see me. ~God

5: Amos predicts a famine for hearing the word of the Lord. Sadly, they didn't have Twitter back then. We are truly privileged.

6: G: "Dear Israel, reclining on your fancy bed, putting on fine lotion, strumming your harp and eating lamb: *You. Are. History*."

7: Amos was once a shepherd and a dresser of sycamore trees. Why don't we dress sycamores nowadays? Who wants naked trees?

8: Amos indicts Wall Street fat cats who make money on the backs of those who punch a Sabbathless 24/7 time card. #occupybible

9: Surprisingly, the book ends with the tiniest shred of hope. G seeks restoration of Israel. Prophet seeks therapist.

OBADIAH

Overview: "Damn those Edomites! We hate those pesky Edomites. We spit on them. Phtew!" Yep, that's the whole book, the shortest in the OT.

1: A one-chapter rant against Edomites. "When will G get rid of them? Say, did you hear we hate Edomites?" Yeah, we deduced that, thanks.

JONAH

Overview: A whale of a tale. Intended as a pious novel and not factual history, but who cares? Everyone loves a fish story.

1: Lesson 1: Don't run from G, who has storms and whales at his disposal. Lesson 2: A few days in a fish can drastically change your outlook.

2: There are no atheists in whalebelly foxholes. Jonah prays and the fish barfs him up on shore. Oh, *now* he'll go to Nineveh.

3: Ninevites learn their city will be toast in forty days, and oddly, they actually repent. G's moved to mercy. No brimstone today!

4: Jonah is ticked that 120,000 Ninevites won't be killed. He wants to die rather than look stupid. Too late. Plus he smells like fish puke.

MICAH

> **Overview:** Do justice. Really, that's it. Stop screwing the poor. Love God and neighbor. Tune out Fox News.

1: G promises that all the Gordon Gekkos in Greedville will lose everything; everybody in Bullytown will feel the whip. Payback's a . . .

2: The rich tell Micah to shut his trap already: "We're the good guys! God's on our side, remember?" Right. Good luck with that.

3: If a prophet takes your money and says you're amazing . . . fraud alert! Real prophets have mood disorders and lecture you for free.

4: After G's temple is restored, we'll sit under our own vine and fig tree, take up farming, and close down West Point. Kumbaya . . .

Under our own vine and fig tree.
Er, palm tree.

5: O Little Town of Bethlehem: Someday you'll be the Messiah's hometown! So deck the halls and belt those Christmas carols.

6: To be in the Justice League, you have to 1) do justice, 2) love kindness, and 3) walk humbly with your G. Capes are optional.

7: "Who is a god like you, G?" (As a hint, the correct answer is "no one." G loves these rhetorical questions. Just humor him.)

NAHUM

Overview: Death to Nineveh. Doom to Nineveh. Mayhem to Nineveh. Babylon will crush it . . . and we bought front-row seats! #gloating

1: G's a jealous god, an Avenger, an angry god, an Avenger, and also an Avenger. (Coming soon to theaters. Joss Whedon not included.)

2: Babylon's attack on Nineveh reads like every gory battle scene in *Game of Thrones*. This is why the Bible can only be shown on HBO.

3: Nineveh's infants are slaughtered, its nobles made slaves, and its corpses stacked high. Just another happy day in Bibleland.

Recess with Judah and Nineveh

HABAKKUK

Overview: A Q and A between a disgruntled customer and the God he doesn't quite understand. Wow, I can totally relate to this book.

1: Hab lobs 20 questions at G. "Why do the righteous suffer? Where is justice? Why do you go AWOL? And why hasn't Godiva been invented yet?"

2: G takes Hab's rebuke surprisingly well. Claims he's working on the problem and that customer service will be back online soon.

3: Hab's so thrilled to have his complaints addressed that he bursts into song. Responsive customer service can do that.

ZEPHANIAH

Overview: G swears he will sweep all creation from the earth. He's got an enormous Swiffer and he's not afraid to use it.

1: The Day of the Lord is at hand! And not in a shiny, happy "Jesus is coming" way. This is more of a "your ass is grass" way.

2: G lays out the judgments for various nations. If you're expecting VIP treatment, Judah, you're delusional. Again.

3: Someday, Judah's remnant will return to G. Until then he'll inhale the scent of her pillow occasionally with a stab of regret.

HAGGAI

Overview: HGTV series about a prophet-turned-contractor with just 3.5 months to rebuild G's temple. But workers are not motivated.

1: Destitute Judeans return from exile and start building houses to live in, but the prophet nags them to finish the temple first. Old Hag.

2: The old folks who remember the first temple think its replacement is shoddy postwar construction. Does *Holmes on Homes* do temples?

ZECHARIAH

Overview: Zech focuses on rebuilding the temple and Israel's fragile self-esteem. Meanwhile, G continues to struggle with bipolar episodes.

1: Four Horsemen of the Apocalypse make a cameo appearance. Hey, they're not supposed to show up until Revelation! That's cheating.

2: The rebuilt city of Jerusalem will soon be overcrowded with people and animals. The OT actually considers this a nice problem to have.

3: High priest Joshua gets an angelic makeover with fresh temple robes. Attention, fashionistas: You can now wear white after Labor Day.

4: G wakes Zech up in the middle of the night for a vision. Couldn't this golden lampstand thingy wait until morning? *Zzzzz.*

5: What's that in the sky—a bird? A plane? NO. It's a thirty-foot flying scroll that says we're doomed. G's not one for subtle gestures.

6: Joshua gets the crown, reigning as both high priest and interim king until the Messiah shows up. I think that's called double dipping.

7: People ask about ritual, but G says they're missing the whole point of religion: justice. Same old, same old. We never learn.

8: G: "I know I was harsh with your ancestors—all that death and exile. But I've mellowed a lot, really. Less with the smiting."

9: Rejoice greatly, O daughter of Zion! Your king's coming. On his way as we speak. He's riding a donkey, so he's just a bit delayed is all.

10: G's rounding up the Ten Lost Tribes from the first exile. Insert your conspiracy theory here about their present whereabouts.

11: Being a softer, more sensitive deity these last few chapters has been hard on G, who's back with the smiting. Maybe it's just his nature.

12: OK, G's thinking positively again. Sorry about chapter 11. He's aiming for continuous improvement at unleashing ruin on our enemies!

13: Uh oh, G's having another dark day. Says he'll slaughter two-thirds of Israel and kill all its prophets. Get him some lithium, stat.

14: Whew, G's back on our side. Zech finishes with a grand vision of G marching out to battle for us. Apparently the lithium helped.

MALACHI

Overview: The OT closes with a court case between an angry nation and the god it's suing for neglect. Pass the chips; this ought to be good.

1: G: "Israelites do white elephant giving, only sacrificing what they don't want themselves. But I don't want another lava lamp!"

2: Plaintiff Israel can't get a word in edgewise as G calls her a liar, a cheater, and a whiner. I know you are, but what am I?

3: G's sending a messenger. But who may abide the day of his coming? Be afraid. He's going to scrub us with a giant Mr. Clean Magic Eraser.

4: The OT ends, ushering in 400 years of silence because G is busy having brain surgery to change his violent personality for the NT.

New Testament

MATTHEW

Overview: "Just in case you missed it, JESUS IS THE MESSIAH OF THE JEWS. And Christ, it's about time he showed up."

1: Just when you thought we'd left the OT, here's a string of begats to put you at ease. Ancestry.com says JC's descended from David. Woot!

2: Astrologers are sent on a field trip to find a Messiah child somewhere out west. "A 'star' . . . um, could you be more specific?"

The Christmas Story

Wise men and shepherds, angels and donkeys. Few New Testament stories are more beloved than the one about Jesus' birth. Or, more accurately, the ones about Jesus' birth, because there are two and they're pretty different. So take a closer look at Matthew 2 and Luke 2. Then listen to what Timothy Beal, author of *Biblical Literacy*, says about the Nativity.

Do you notice anything missing here [in Matthew]? Where's the annunciation to Mary by the angel Gabriel? What about Mary's visit to Elizabeth? The birth of John the Baptist? No room in the inn? Away in a manger? Shepherds watching flocks by night? None of that is part of this story. That's all in the Gospel of Luke. In fact, the story of Jesus' birth that most of us know from "The Little Drummer Boy" and Christmas pageants is an amalgam of Matthew and Luke, bringing together characters and events from both gospels into one story.

What we do see in Matthew's Nativity are things that point to Jesus as a Messiah and king. Not for Matthew are lowly shepherds the first to hear the news, or poverty-stricken parents forced to give birth in a stable. After opening with a substantial genealogical detour to demonstrate Jesus' Davidic street cred, Matthew immediately places him as a "king of the Jews" who is feared by other kings. A king needs to be visited by dignitaries, so Matthew is the gospel that shows the wise men/magi not only visiting Jesus—then probably approaching two years of age—but kneeling before him. (The gospel never calls them kings, by the way, or claims that there were three of them.)

What's important about understanding these early differences in Matthew and Luke is that they are signposts to show us what will be emphasized throughout each gospel. Matthew is generally going to emphasize continuity with Jewish tradition and keep a focus on Jesus as the king of the Jews, the fulfillment of prophecy. Luke, by contrast, is far more interested in spreading the gospel beyond the Jews to include Gentiles and God knows who else.

3: John the Baptist prepares the way by baptizing JC and anticipating the organic food movement. Locusts + honey = delish.

4: JC's chapter checklist: Get tempted by Satan. Transform 12 losers into disciples. Launch universal health care. Quote OT when possible.

5: JC's Greatest Hits include "Beatitudes," "You Are Salt," and "Don't Even Think about Adultery or You've Already Committed It."

6: Don't store up your treasures on earth. Get a safety deposit box in heaven and put your heart in it. Metaphorically speaking.

7: Dear judgmental hypocrite: You probably haven't noticed, but there's a big honkin' plank in your eye. You might want to remove it.

8: JC heals Peter's MIL so she can fix him some supper. At least he doesn't also have her fetch him a beer while he watches TV.

9: JC explicitly orders two guys not to tell anybody that he just healed them of blindness. Apparently they were also deaf, however.

10: The 12 get promoted to new job title of "apostles." No extra pay, but they receive cool new superpowers. Some travel required.

11: JC and JnBap are chided for not joining in the crowd's reindeer games. JnBap's too pious and JC's not pious enough. They just can't win.

12: JC tells Pharisees to lighten up about the Sabbath, which is a message so dangerous they plot to kill him. Just not on the Sabbath.

13: The 12 ask JC why he speaks to the people in parables. They'd prefer straightforward behavioral checklists, please. With maps.

14: Salome gets JnBap's head on a platter! This nummy tale whets our appetite for the next story: Feeding the five thousand. Pass the chips?

15: Pharisees are mad that the 12 don't wash hands before meals. Even Pharisee preschoolers wash while singing "Happy Birthday" to the end.

16: Spoiler alert! JC says he'll go to Jerusalem, suffer terribly, die, and rise again. The 12 want a new script with less trauma.

17: After a mountaintop transfiguration, JC no longer has to send his robes out for bleaching. Also, his face is all shiny-happy.

18: If your eye makes trouble, gouge it out. (Disclaimer: *The Twible* is not liable for any maimings that result from biblical literalism.)

19: JC says it's easier to thread a needle with a thick rope than for the rich to get into heaven. And we've botched that verse ever since.

20: Workers in a vineyard sue the boss for unpredictable labor practices. Oddly, JC sides with management. I'm more for the workers, myself.

21: JC curses a perfectly innocent fig tree. What did that tree ever do to him? Now it can never become a Fig Newton.

22: The kingdom of heaven is like when Emeril prepares a rockin' feast and invites every homeless street person in NOLA. Jumbo gumbo = yum.

23: "Woe to the Pharisees!" Which, if you read closer, probably means you. How's that gnat-straining working out for you?

24: JC says the signs of the end will include war, earthquake, and famine. Which pretty much describes every single year of human history.

25: Calling all sheep! All sheep, head this way to heaven! Thanks for feeding and clothing the poor. P.S. Sorry, goats, you're on your own.

Salome felt like her birthday came early that year.

The Sheep and the Goats

Matthew 25 is one of those chapters that most of us would like to soften. Or ignore entirely. The climax of the chapter is a vision of the end times, when Jesus separates the sheep (those who have fed the hungry, clothed the naked, visited the imprisoned, etc.) from the goats (those who preferred watching other people do good deeds on TV). The chapter puts forward the unforgettable idea that whatever we do to one another, for good or for ill, we are actually doing to Christ. What's more, our sins of omission are just as damning as any wickedness we could actively pursue.

I should tell you, on a personal note, that this passage has long scared the pants off me. I am not a biblical literalist—which will not come as a shock to you at this juncture, three-quarters of the way through *The Twible*—but if there is a fire-and-brimstone passage I take literally, it would be this one.

It's all quite terrifying, to tell you the truth.

So this seems like a good place to mention that a quarter of all author proceeds from this book are being donated to five different charities that practice humanitarian aid, and that one of them is Matthew 25 Ministries. See the acknowledgments at the end of this book for more information.

26: Rough night. Judas betrays Jesus and the other 11 fall asleep during his darkest hour. They had overloaded on carbs at the Last Supper.

27: After being tried and mocked, JC's crucified on the cross. "Eli, Eli, lema sabachthani?" Even JC can feel distant from G.

28: JC rises from dead—stronger and now with more salvific staying power! Guards improvise a CYA story to explain how they lost his body.

MARK

Overview: Beta version of the gospel. No resurrection story in original due to data loss. ☹ This bug was fixed later by Matt and Luke OS. ☺

1: JC calls fishermen to be his disciples and become "fishers of men." But will the people they catch taste as good as the fish?

2: Don't pour new wine in old wineskins. The skins will burst and you'll lose all that awesome wine. Which is a bona fide biblical sin.

3: A house divided against itself cannot stand. Say, for example, one person roots for Michigan and another for Ohio State. Hypothetically.

4: VBS Parables: "The kingdom of God is like a mustard seed. No, kids, never*mind* that mustard tastes icky. That's really not the point."

5: JC raises a girl from the dead! Good thing she was just 12. If she'd been a teen, she would have slept all day until *she* wanted to get up.

6: JC walks on water like it's no big deal, but the 12 are ready to call the Ghostbusters and Channel 5 News. They get jumpy sometimes.

7: After missing the point yet again, the 12 receive a set of "I'm with stupid" t-shirts. They're just dumb enough to be excited.

8: Jesus heals a blind man who then claims to see people who resemble walking trees. So now the guy can see, but he's high on drugs.

9: An anxious dad wants JC to heal his son, crying, "I believe . . . help thou my unbelief!" Massive brownie points for your honesty, pal.

10: JC tells a rich young man to sell it all and donate to charity, but he goes AWOL from the Bible instead. Downward mobility's unpopular.

11: Jerusalem treats the newly arrived JC like a rock star. Sure, they're going to kill him in a few days, but why spoil the moment?

12: JC says it's kosher to pay taxes to Caesar. This is the IRS's favorite chapter of the Bible. The rest of us aren't too thrilled with it.

13: The end times will feature an ultra-cheery scenario where parents kill their kids and vice versa. The NT's as family friendly as the OT.

14: Hours after swearing they'd die before leaving JC, the 12 run for the hills when he's arrested. With friends like these . . .

15: In the climactic finale of *Survivor: Jerusalem*, bloodthirsty viewers vote to free Barabbas and boot JC off the island. Ratings soar.

16: The original gospel stops right before the resurrection, but first-century test audiences cry out for a happier ending and more popcorn.

The Beta Version of Mark

Despite their many differences, one thing all four gospels have in common is their climactic accounts of Jesus' resurrection. But while Mark's gospel contains such a story *now*, the earliest surviving manuscripts of it do not. Mark's story originally ended at 16:8 with the women arriving on the scene to find the tombstone rolled away and a strange young man dressed in white outside the tomb. He tells them that Jesus will catch up with them later and instructs them to pass it on to Peter, but the women never actually see the risen Jesus or enter the tomb. The gospel's final verse has them fleeing the scene in fear.

Why did the earliest versions of this gospel only imply the resurrection and not depict it outright? The more prosaic theories have "Mark," or whoever authored this gospel, stepping out for the first-century equivalent of a cup of coffee and thereby allowing the last page of his manuscript to blow away or be eaten by wolves. Since Mark had not backed up the most recent version of the document in his Dropbox, the argument goes, the gospel's ending was lost.

I don't find this to be terribly persuasive because everything else about Mark's gospel strikes me as carefully plotted and deliberate. He is an intentional narrator, his spare prose rarely displaying emotion and giving nothing away about himself. There is no fluff of any kind in Mark, and his very omissions are significant.

The late novelist and Duke professor Reynolds Price has a hypothesis I find far more compelling. "Mark intended to end his story as we have it, in literal midair while the women flee the tomb in terror," he writes. "Such an apparently reckless last-minute abandonment by an author of his reader's keenest final expectation is thoroughly characteristic of the kind of narrator Mark has been throughout his book. This is my story, suddenly told—you tell it from here."

In other words, Mark intentionally left his gospel open-ended because he wants us to live out the story. We are the women who discover the empty tomb—will we panic? Spread the news? What will we do next?

LUKE

Overview: The gospel that cares about women, the poor, and the marginalized. FYI, Luke has recently been banned by the Tea Party.

1: Teen girl Mary chosen by G to bear the Savior! OK, the pregnancy raises some eyebrows, but a double thumbs up to Joseph for loyalty.

2: "Ma'am, the rooms are full at Bethlehem Inn, but there's a rustic barn out back that is quite charming. And the hay is complimentary."

3: JnBap preaches that if you have two coats, you should give one away. He donated both of his, which explains the whole loincloth look.

4: Sword drill! JC and Satan one-up each other quoting Bible verses. It's like a wilderness forerunner to fundamentalist Bible camp.

5: Luke introduces the Pharisees, who cross-examine JC about the law. Cause the Pharisees aren't fair, you see. [Cue thunder.]

The Gospel of the Margins

Jesus opens his public ministry with a flourish by heading to his hometown synagogue in Nazareth and teaching the people (Luke 4: 14–30). "Oh, how sweet!" they might have said. "Joseph and Mary's little boy is back for a visit, all grown up and ready to teach us the Torah. Let's pinch his cheeks!"

But this is not in fact what goes down. Jesus teaches in the temple all right, recounting two seemingly innocuous stories they would have all been familiar with—one of Elijah healing a widow and another of Elisha healing a leper.

And then the people try to kill him. Yes, that's right, the very same small-town people who knew his parents and watched him grow up drag him out of the synagogue and up to the top of a mountain. From there they attempt to hurl him to his death. He only barely escapes.

Um, what just happened?

The key to understanding this story is hidden in the Hebrew Bible/Old Testament. Jesus could have chosen any number of texts to preach on, but in selecting stories about prophets who went out of their way to help non-Israelites, he was sending a clear message: You people are no longer the only game in God's town. In his commentary *Luke for Everyone,* the incomparable N.T. Wright summarizes the passage this way:

> Elijah was sent to help a widow—but not a Jewish one. Elisha healed one solitary leper—and the leper was the commander of the enemy army. That's what did it. That's what drove them to fury. Israel's God was rescuing the wrong people.

Jesus' religious contemporaries in the first century were expecting much more justice than this. After everything they had suffered under centuries of political oppressors, they wanted a Messiah who would kick those oppressors the hell out of their land, not add more leaves to the table and invite the jerks to dinner.

6: "Don't judge; pray for your enemies; bless those who curse you." Talk about high expectations. I prefer a good imprecatory psalm, thanks.

7: A prostitute crashes a dinner party to love on JC, who says she actually has better manners than his Pharisee host. ShutDOWN.

8: A woman is healed from 12 years of bleeding just by touching the hem of JC's cloak. So *this* is why superheroes need capes.

9: JC predicts his death (twice!) but the 12 don't pay attention because they're having a thrilling argument about who's greatest. Sheesh.

10: Outcast Samaritan aids an injured man who's been left for dead by the religious establishment. They then name 8,628 hospitals after him.

11: MaryBeth studies at Jesus University to become a teacher, upsetting her sister Martha, who wants her to major in home economics.

12: The 12 excel as weathermen but fail to read the signs of the times. Still, with better hair they'll be sure to get jobs in TV news.

13: JC says he tried to be all mother-hennish and take us under his wing, but we rebelled and insisted on becoming free-range chicks.

14: JC: "Wanna be a disciple? Hate your family, sell your stuff, and lay down your life! Just sign here . . . wait, where are you going?"

15: Dad welcomes his prodigal son back home with open arms and no questions asked, forever raising parenting standards for the rest of us.

The Pharisees

Most people today equate "Pharisees" with "bad guys of the New Testament." That's because the gospels show the Pharisees as hard and inflexible enforcers of religious orthodoxy, always stalking Jesus to catch him in some blunder or other. If he heals on the Sabbath or breaks the purity laws, he's a blasphemer who should be punished by the religious community. If he talks smack about the Roman Empire, he's a traitor who should be executed by the state. The Pharisees don't seem to care whether they trip Jesus up on religion or politics, just as long as they catch him red-handed doing *something* wrong.

But in the context of first-century Judaism, the Pharisees were just one of several religious sects, and the word "Pharisee" was not yet synonymous with "tightass." Pharisees differed from the Sadducees, a rival Jewish sect, because they believed in a physical resurrection of the body in the world to come. They differed from the Zealots because they rejected violent revolution as the preferred means of getting Rome off their backs. And they differed from the Essenes because they just weren't the types to turn their backs on the world and go live in caves. Not that there's anything wrong with that, you understand. Caves are terrific. But the Pharisees, unlike the Essenes, were fully invested in the temple cult of urban Judaism, so retreating from that world in favor of an ascetic cave-dwelling hermithood was not their scene.

In their own day, the Pharisees were actually pretty popular, since they were more in tune with ordinary people than the wealthy Sadducees or the austere Essenes. They emphasized ways of living the law that regular folks could apply to their lives, work, and families. And if the Pharisees sometimes went over the top in their zeal for correct behavior, it might have been because they were well versed in the Scriptures and knew exactly what had happened centuries before when their ancestors had strayed from the path.

16: A man who was rich and arrogant in life finds that in the afterlife he's a homeless beggar. This would make an *awesome* reality TV show.

17: Bible math: 70 x 7 = 490. The limit on forgiving? JC says no, which means the math lesson was bogus from the start. Class dismissed.

18: A persistent widow hounds a judge to stop delaying her court case. Victory! The squeaky wheel always gets the grease.

19: Fanboy Zacchaeus scrambles up a tree just to ask JC to dinner. Dude, your underwear's showing. Next time use Evite.

20: Tenants Behaving Badly. A landlord is sad when tenants kill his servants and his only son. Hmm, Bible . . . foreshadowing much?

21: A poor widow gives every last coin while the rich cough up only a little of their wealth. Not much has changed since the first century.

22: It's the Last Supper, JC's about to die, and the 12 are *still* fighting about which among them is the greatest. Can we smack them now?

23: There's just nothing funny about Jesus dying on a cross. Sorry. Catch up with me in the next chapter.

24: The 12 don't believe Mary and the other women when they bring the good news that JC is risen. I still want, quite badly, to slap the 12.

JOHN

Overview: The weirdest of the Bible's four gospels is parable-free and trades in dualism: light/dark, good/evil, Apple/Google. (Go 🍎.)

1: No manger story, no wise men: "The Word was G and the Word was with G." Great. We're only "in the beginning" and it's incomprehensible.

2: JC starts his ministry by turning water into wine, forever silencing all those who would dismiss his followers as killjoys.

3: G so loved the world that he sent his only Son. To save the WORLD, not just you and the people who agree with you. OK, rant over.

4: JC promises a woman she'll never thirst again if she drinks his living water. It has more electrolytes than Gatorade. Patent pending.

5: JC orders a paralytic to get up and walk. Hey, this approach could solve our health care crisis! Just *tell* folks not to be sick.

6: "Taste of Galilee" is a hit when JC feeds 5,000 people with five loaves and two fish. Can he also multiply chocolate cake for dessert?

7: JC's brothers urge him to attend a festival to show off his miracles and get all famous, but that's just not his style. He's on the QT.

8: DVD release of John contains a deleted scene that wasn't in the original gospel: JC saving a woman caught in adultery. *Love* that scene.

9: JC uses his own saliva to heal a man born blind, so the first thing the guy sees is a stranger spitting on him. Hello, cruel world.

10: JC says he is the Good Shepherd who lays down his life for the sheep. The Bad Shepherd just eats the sheep. Mmm, mutton.

11: The only NT example of JC crying is when his pal Lazarus dies. He also cries when the Reds lose, but it's not recorded in the Bible.

12: Since JC can raise folks from the tomb, the Phars want to send *him* to a tomb. It's the Law of Conservation of Dead People.

13: The 12 freak out when JC wants to wash their feet, but at least he doesn't use his own spit this time. That's progress.

14: JC says he's the way to the Father, but it's all a bit vague. Doubting Tom: "Lord, we have no GPS. How will we find you?"

15: JC: "Love one another as I have loved you." It's really not much to ask, you know; just be willing to die for others. Oh. There's that.

16: G: "You haven't asked for squat. Ask and ye shall receive." So . . . NOW can I have a pony? I've been begging you ever since Psalm 5!

17: JC prays that all his followers will have unity and harmony. This prayer will be answered at such time as hell freezes over.

18: A posse of soldiers, priests, and random cowboy extras come to arrest JC, who prefers to go quietly despite Pete's gun-blazing tactics.

19: Even while dying on a cross, JC makes arrangements for his mom to go live with John. That's some serious grace under pressure.

20: Doubting Tom mauls JC's wounds to make sure his resurrection's the real deal. JC: "Ouch. Couldn't you just take my word for it?"

21: JC to Pete: "Do you love me with agape love?" Pete: "Sure! I friended you three times on Facebook." JC: "Fair enough. Feed my lambs."

What Kind of Love?

"**S**imon son of John, do you love me more than these?" Jesus asks Peter in John 21. Peter hastily assures Jesus that *of course*, despite the whole "I just denied you three times" thing, Peter loves him like crazy. It's an odd conversation, because Jesus keeps repeating the same question and Peter keeps replying the same way: "Yes, Lord, you know that I love you." Peter seems a little put out that Jesus would continue asking the question three times—which is exactly the number of times that Peter had denied knowing him. Clearly, it's redemption time.

But the conversation Peter and Jesus are having is more complex than our English translations would suggest. Biblical Greek has four different words for love, and the kind of love Jesus is asking for and the kind of love Peter offers to Jesus are not the same thing. Jesus wants to know if Peter feels *agape* for him— *agape* being the full, charitable love that God has for humanity. Peter responds instead that he feels he and Jesus are BFFs. In his commentary on the Gospel of John, Mark Matson writes,

> The first term is Jesus' usual term for love, used throughout the Gospel, and refers to a selfless love often associated with God's love toward people; the second term is a common term for brotherly love, but it also implies self-giving and consideration of the other first.

Matson feels that the *phileo* love that Peter offers instead of the *agape* love that Jesus is asking for is not necessarily a lesser commitment. However, it's significant that when Jesus asks Peter the third and final time "Do you love me?" he meets Peter on his own terms. Jesus doesn't repeat the request for *agape* but asks if Peter regards him with the love of a friend. He already knows that Peter does, since he was listening to Peter's answers the first two times. But perhaps he wants Peter to feel he's been met halfway, and that whatever love Peter is capable of offering is acceptable in God's sight. In any case, the task before Peter is the same: to feed the lambs and tend the sheep.

ACTS

Overview: Paul's missionary travels as recounted years later in a church basement with a slide projector and non-kosher snacks.

1: Disciple National Convention meets in Jerusalem to elect Matthias as newest member of the 12. (The vacancy was due to a scandal. Ssssh.)

2: Product launch: Holy Ghost language course. Better than Berlitz! [Warning: User may seem inebriated. Tongue may catch fire.]

3: Pete tests his new healing powers to help a lame homeless dude perform an Irish jig into the temple gates. Biblical Riverdance!

4: The earliest Christians share everything in common, redistributing their wealth and property according to need. Bloody socialists.

5: A married couple withholds money from the commune and then both fall down dead. Moral? Next time they pass the plate at church . . .

6: Stephen's seized for talking smack about how Jesus is going to destroy the temple and the law. Them's fightin' words, you blasphemer.

7: Stephen's sermon. Social hint: it's not very diplomatic to call your accusers stiff-necked, uncircumcised murderers. Stoning may result.

8: An Ethiopian eunuch tries to understand the OT without a teacher, but Philip says to just read *The Twible* instead. It's so much shorter.

9: JC to Saul in vision: "Just wondering. Why are you killing off my followers?" Saul: "Oops, Lord. I'll stop now. Wow, you're shiny!"

10: During noon prayers, Pete has a trippy vision of unclean animals now becoming kosher. That's good news for Christians; bacon is tasty.

11: Pete explains his vision and announces that 1) keeping kosher is *so* yesterday and 2) G actually cares about Gentiles. It's news to him.

12: An angel helps Pete with a daring nighttime prison escape, then strikes Herod dead on the throne. Way to angelically multitask.

Peter's tasty, tasty vision

 ACTS **239**

13: Paul (was Saul) is the Rick Steves of the NT world, except he tells people they're ungodly and doesn't care if their paella's delicious.

14: Paul gets stoned and exiled by an angry mob, but he's up and preaching again the very next day. Talk about a strong work ethic.

15: Paul says adult male converts don't have to get the snip-snip treatment. Guys, you can uncross your legs now. It's going to be OK.

16: Since it's always wise to return to the same city that recently tried to stone you, Paul goes to Lystra. He's determined, our Paul.

17: In Athens, Paul argues Greek philosophy, then takes everybody out for gyros and baklava. Nah. Actually he just lectures them.

18: Paul stays in Corinth a record 18 months, and this time it's not even because he's in jail. He must enjoy all that bracing sea air.

19: Paul's handkerchiefs are so holy that people get healed just from touching them. That's some seriously powerful snot.

20: During Paul's day-long sermon, Eutychus dozes off, falls through a window, and dies. Paul might want to try doing a TED talk next time.

Know the Book of Acts

How well do you know the Book of Acts? Check to see if you've been paying attention or if you, like the ill-fated Eutychus of chapter 20, fell asleep somewhere along the way.

Acts was likely written by the same person who wrote the Gospel of
- **a)** Mark
- **b)** Luke
- **c)** Mary

A major theme of the Book of Acts is the apostles taking the gospel to the
- **a)** Gentiles
- **b)** Brits
- **c)** Little people

After Stephen's sermon, the people decide to
- **a)** Convert to Christianity
- **b)** Go out for falafel
- **c)** Stone Stephen, and then go out for falafel

When Paul goes to Mars Hill, his sermon shows that
- **a)** He has taken the time to study Greek philosophy
- **b)** He thinks the Greek philosophers are full of crap
- **c)** Both A and B

The Book of Acts ends with
- **a)** Paul's beheading (very exciting!)
- **b)** Paul's court trial (zzzzz . . .)
- **c)** Paul's latest argument with Peter

Answers are in the "Acts" section of the notes at the back of the book. There is a reward there for five correct answers.

21: Paul's PR problems intensify when he's accused of bringing non-Jews into the Jerusalem temple. The whole city's in an uproar. Fun times.

22: Speaking as his own defense counsel, Paul stresses his Jewish street cred and recounts his conversion story to the pissed-off crowd.

23: Paul makes a shameless play for Pharisee sympathy, so now only the Sadducees want to kill him. Divide and conquer; that's how it's done.

24: Paul in court: "I'm just a good Jew who came to Jerusalem to make offerings in the temple. Why do they hate me so much? Boo hoo."

25: It's two years later and Paul's *still* arguing his court case. Romans invented bureaucracy alongside convenient roads and the aqueduct.

26: And . . . again with the conversion story. This time Paul claims that G promised to deliver him from the Jewish people. How convenient.

27: Paul's case is remanded to Rome, but . . . shipwreck! Paul had warned the crew about it, so he has a satisfying "I told you so" moment.

28: Paul stops earning Frequent Sailor Miles after a last stop in Rome. Acts' beheading finale was too sad, so it was cut. No pun intended.

ROMANS

Overview: Paul's magnum opus covers grace, law, faith, sin, and salvation. Clearly, people don't write letters like they used to.

1: Paul's opening comments to this church make one thing clear: When in Rome, do not do as the Romans do. Idols = bad.

2: It turns out that merely being circumcised isn't enough to assure salvation. Really sorry for that inconvenience, Jewish male readers.

3: "No one is righteous. Nobody understands G. Works and knowledge won't save you." Well, then. I guess I'll just play Nintendo.

4: "Abraham's an exemplar of faith!" Here Paul ignores Gen 12:13, 17:17, and 20:11. But it's kinda nice when our worst moments are forgotten.

5: "Suffering builds endurance, which creates character, which brings hope!" Suffering also brings whining and angst; see *Book of Job, The*.

Paul on Amazing Grace

If a single word could sum up Paul's theology, it would be grace. Grace as in, "I didn't earn my salvation, and am in fact a scumbag, but God rescued me." Throughout his letters, and perhaps especially here in Romans, Paul lays out a variety of things that cannot save us:

- Keeping the law can't save us. (Are you listening to this, Galatians?)
- Being born into a particular tribe of Israel can't save us.
- Having proper knowledge of God or doctrine can't save us.
- Being circumcised can't save us.
- Our good deeds can't save us.
- Thor can't save us.

The one thing that *can* save us is the one thing we cannot engineer for ourselves: God's grace. Paul says this grace is freely given to everyone apart from the law.

Does that mean that since grace abounds, we have a get-out-of-sin-free card and can do whatever the hell we want? "By no means!" thunders Uncle Paul. "How can we who died to sin go on living in it?" If you read Paul's letters you'll find he's no softy on sin. In fact, he spends a good deal of time calling out sins in the diverse churches under his care and expressing keen disappointment that the people don't seem to be any better behaved than their pagan counterparts. In 1 Corinthians 5, Paul even says the church in Corinth is actually *worse* than pagan, because at least the pagans have sense enough to know that having sex with one's stepmother is rarely a good idea.

So the fine line in reading Paul is always in grasping on the one hand that godly behavior is paramount (something the Corinthians never understood) even while knowing that such behavior won't save you (something the Galatians never understood). Complicating matters still further is the fact that Paul's radical views on grace weren't always accepted by other prominent leaders in the first-century church, especially James.

6: "We used to be slaves to sin, but now we get to be slaves to righteousness." The new slavery's much better. Trust Uncle Paul on this.

7: "I do the thing I don't want to do and don't do the thing I want to do." That pretty much encapsulates all of life. And dieting.

8: All things work together for good for those who love G. Except, of course, when they don't. But it's a great theory in the abstract.

9: Paul teaches that we are predestined to have free will. After writing this, his brain detonates from Irony Overload.

10: "Everyone who calls on the name of the Lord will be saved." Even people I don't like? What kind of crap religion is this? Grace for all?

11: G starts handing out backstage salvation passes to *hoi polloi*. So much for being the few, the proud, the chosen people.

12: "If your enemies are hungry, feed them; if they thirst, give them drink." Is it OK to spit in the drink first? Just asking.

13: Paul says we should submit to government leaders in authority, for they are G's chosen servants. Tyrants throughout history rejoice.

14: Do not judge one another. Even when someone really, really deserves it. Maybe especially then. Be like a duck.

15: You know how at the end of a long letter, someone might drop a hint that they'd like to come visit? Paul does that here. Subtle.

16: "Hi, Junia, you totally awesome woman apostle. Hi, Phoebe and Mary and Prisca. Chicks rule. Thanks for your help. Love ya! –Paul."

1 CORINTHIANS ✝

Overview: Don't fight. Don't have sex. Don't worship idols. Don't have sex. And did you catch the "no sex" part? Just checking.

1: Paul's Jewish mom skillz: "I loved you and taught you, so how could you shame me like this? Where'd I go wrong? Here, eat some soup."

2: Paul preaches not with wise words, but by demonstrating the Holy Spirit's power. This may or may not involve magic tricks.

3: "Don't say 'I'm with Paul' or 'I'm with Apollos.' You're with Jesus now, people. Those t-shirts were meant to be ironic."

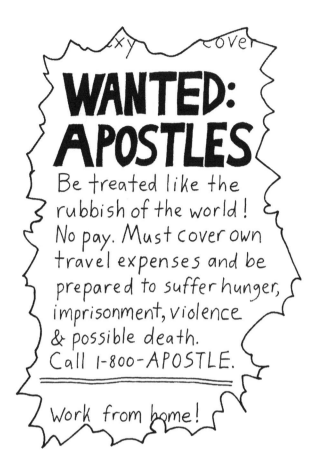

4: Wanted: Apostles. Unpaid jobs require travel with no T & E budget. You may be assaulted, spat upon, or killed in action. Apply within.

5: "Stop having 50 shades of sex. Also, forget all I said about not judging. Go right ahead and condemn your oversexed neighbor."

6: Paul rails against so-called Christians who sue each other in court. The Bible sure can feel awfully relevant two thousand years later.

7: Paul reserves the domain name YouShouldStaySingle.com to show that marriage is overrated, but folks still prefer hooking up.

The Love Chapter

So, you're at another wedding, and you can pretty much predict how the ceremony will unfold. To be reflective and cultured, the bride and groom will have chosen a reading from Shakespeare's 116th Sonnet. To be inclusive and culturally relevant, there will then be a passage from *The Prophet* by Kahlil Gibran. And then, no matter how nontraditional the wedding may be in other ways, someone will read 1 Corinthians 13.

That's because 1 Corinthians 13 is one of the Bible's most beautiful ruminations on love. Not gushy romantic love, which is about having a *Jerry Maguire*-esque "You complete me" fulfillment of the self, but an in-the-trenches love that places other people's interests before our own. Paul says that such love is not puffed up with pride—which is what he's accused the Corinthians of being all throughout this letter—but humble and gracious.

New Testament scholar N.T. Wright says it's important to position the famous love passage in the context of the chapters immediately before and after it, making chapters 12 to 14 a literary unit that is concerned with how people are meant to live together as the body of Christ. Paul claims that none of the great things we can *do* for Christ—giving away all our money, martyring our bodies to the cause, preaching the coolest sermons—amount to a hill of beans if we don't have love. Wright says, "Love is God's river, flowing on into the future, across the border into the country where there is no pride, no jostling for position, no contention among God's people. We are invited to step into that river here and now, and let it take us where it's going."

So the next time you hear this at a wedding, remember the larger message: all spiritual gifts will someday cease; knowledge will end; the things of this world are a drop in the bucket. All that will remain is love.

8: Paul's fine with eating meat that's been offered to idols. But if YOU have a problem with it, he'll go veggie. Guilt trip much?

9: Paul: "And speaking of meat, did I mention the church forgot to pay or feed me? I have to grab whatever I can, unlike PETER . . ."

10: "Your ancestors loved idols, sex, and nonstop complaining. Do you really want to be like them? P.S. G smote their sorry asses."

11: Paul says we should judge for ourselves whether it's proper for a woman to pray without a veil. Hmmm. I judge yes. Next question?

12: In the body of Christ, every part is vital to the whole. Except our metaphorical appendix. There's really just no point to that.

13: Love is patient and kind. It does not get annoyed or impatient that this chapter is read at Every. Single. Wedding. Love bears all.

14: Paul wants us all to learn to prophesy. I prophesy that this likely will not happen. See, I'm already getting good at it.

15: As Christ was resurrected from the dead, so we will one day be. Just keep an ear out for that trumpet blast, dead people.

16: Paul's final good-byes: "Be good. Send me some money. I'll come visit soon. SWAHK!" (Sealed with a holy kiss.)

2 CORINTHIANS

Overview: The fact that this is called the "severe" letter shows how well Corinth took Paul's advice the first time. Fasten your seat belts.

1: Paul's recent visit to Corinth didn't go well. He says he'll wait a while before trying again. But no hard feelings, right? RIGHT?

2: Paul: "When I write those sad, angry letters it's for your own good. Making you feel awful about yourselves is how I show my love. Xxoo."

3: Paul says the Torah was a "ministry of death" chiseled on stone tablets. You can see why he wasn't always Mr. Popularity with Jews.

4: "We are afflicted but not crushed; perplexed but not despairing; stricken but not destroyed. Thank G for Wellbutrin."

5: "Your body is the tent you live in for now, but after death you'll get keys to your permanent home in heaven. I know tent camping sucks."

6: Paul's life has been full of beatings, jail time, and hunger. It's not all fun and games, being an apostle. You could put an eye out.

7: "So glad you repent of how badly you treated me! All my passive-aggressive letters sure did work. Oh, how I love you. Mwa."

8: Stewardship Sunday. Paul's new guilt tactic: "If penniless Macedonia can cough it up, so can you, rich Corinth." Score.

9: "So . . . I'm sending some guys to collect your entirely voluntary, mind-blowingly generous donations. All major credit cards accepted."

10: Paul raises the bar on the miseries listed in chapter 6: "Shipwrecked three times. Beaten five times. I was even stoned once. Top that!"

11: Paul calls his rivals "super-apostles," which sounds like a compliment but is actually an exemplary case of biblical sarcasm.

12: "Oh, this thorn in my side! I'm in such pain. How I suffer. But enough about me. Have *you* noticed how much I suffer?"

13: "P.S. Corinthians, I rejoice when I'm weak and you're strong. Your perfection is all I've *ever* lived for! But no pressure."

GALATIANS

Overview: You know those pissed-off letters you sometimes write but never actually put in the mail? Well, Paul sent his. Oh boy howdy.

1: You can tell Paul's mad because he won't even say hi. No respects, no holy kisses. It's straight to the woodshed, do not pass go.

2: Paul says that when Peter came to Antioch, they had a blowout fight. Theology throwdown, apostle-style! Wish they'd sold tickets.

3: "You idiot Galatians! What part of 'saved-by-grace-and-not-by-works' did you not understand?" Oh. Pretty much all of it.

Paul

The Stupid, Foolish, Idiotic Galatians Who Probably Won't Even Read This Because They Never Listen To Me Anyway

4: Paul's remedial class takes Galatia back to Genesis for a crash course in law versus freedom: Freedom good. Law not so good.

5: "I wish all those guys who confuse you about the circumcision question would just go castrate themselves already. The dicks."

6: "Don't be weary; don't lose heart; don't give up!" The letter ends merrily as grumpy Paul tries awkward new gig as motivational speaker.

EPHESIANS

Overview: Ephesians is to Galatians as Audrey Hepburn is to Howard Stern. More elegant restraint; less shrill pugilism.

1: Paul has "not ceased in thanksgiving." Apparently no one told him that he can stop eating leftover turkey anytime now.

2: The dead are made alive in Christ, which is sure-fire evidence that there are zombies right there in the Bible.

3: Paul pens a thrilling mystery novel about grace. SPOILER ALERT: The Gentiles get saved at the end. Also, the butler did it.

4: "Don't let the sun go down on your anger." This advice works most realistically if you live in northern Alaska in the summertime.

5: Paul takes it for granted that "no one ever hated their own body." Clearly he was not a 21st-century North American woman.

6: "Children, obey your parents." I'd try to be caustic about this, but I have a teenager, so . . . listen to Uncle Paul, kids.

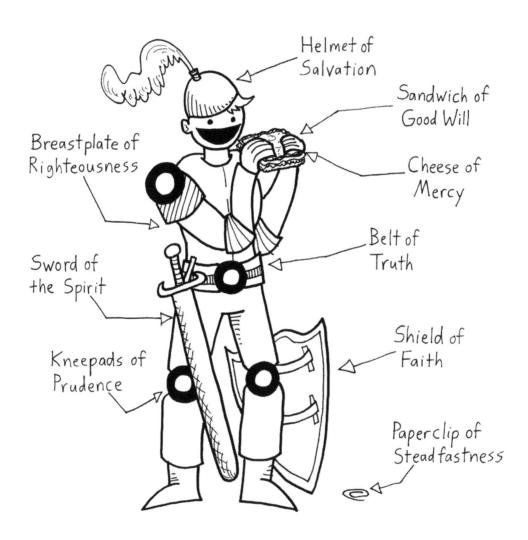

PHILIPPIANS

Overview: It's funny how Paul can only write kind, cheerful letters when he's in jail and needs people to bring him food.

1: Paul's got joy, joy, joy, joy: 17 times in this letter. Man, did he ever take a happy pill since writing to the Galatians.

2: Paul insists the church must always have unity in everything. Thousands of different Christian denominations now agree.

3: Paul says that anything that's not Christ crucified is SHIT. Horrified church translates as "dung" to wash Paul's mouth with soap.

4: "I can do all things thru Christ who strengthens me." Yes, but sometimes this verse is more guilt-inducing than it is inspirational.

COLOSSIANS

Overview: Lessons for New Christians: Follow the master. Be grateful. Obey. Beware of strangers. In other words, be a good dog.

1: "Dear brother and sister in Christ, once you were G's enemies, but now he's rescued you from the Pit of Despair. That's twoo wuvvv."

2: You know how on Mardi Gras, Jesus is buried inside the King Cake? Paul says the gospel is like that. So look out for your dentures.

3: *Extreme Makeover: NT Edition.* If anyone is in Christ, he or she is a new creation. And we're not just talking about better hair.

4: "Masters, provide your slaves with what is right and fair." How about freedom? That seems right and fair.

1 THESSALONIANS

Overview: Paul's earliest letter. He just adored this church, which shows that his crabbiness arose after he was exposed to other Christians.

1: The dead will rise to greet the Lord in the air. To practice for this moment, say "How do you do, Lord?" while levitating.

2: Paul has loved the Thessalonians like a nursing mother loves her baby. And unlike the Galatians, they never gave him mastitis.

3: The Thessalonians' report card. "Faithfulness: A! Cheer in persecution: A! Love for Paul: A!" Clearly, this church is teacher's pet.

4: Just because folks in Thessalonica are thriving doesn't mean Paul doesn't have instructions for them. Warning: wee sermon ahead.

5: Judgment day will come suddenly, so don't be a jerk. G sees you when you're sleeping. He knows when you're awake.

2 THESSALONIANS

Overview: "I know I said that Jesus was coming soon, but that did not mean TODAY. Please don't quit your day job."

PAUL'S CAREER CENTER

Idleness

Earn your keep, and pay your way!

JOB APPLICATION

WORK JOBS

CAREERS

1: "G will shut your enemies out of the kingdom forever. Hooray!" Somehow I don't feel this is the awesome news the author thinks it is.

2: "No, JC has *not* already returned. We have to live through a terrifying tribulation first. So we have that to look forward to."

3: Don't be idle, don't be a moocher, and don't hang out with moochers. They'll eat your chocolate, and that can't be good.

I Timothy

Overview: We now leave Paul to pick up the NT story more than a generation later. Warning: women have not fared very well in the interim.

1: "Stop promoting false doctrine! P.S. Just to clarify, 'false doctrine' is defined as anything I did not teach you myself."

2: "Any woman who presumes to teach men the Bible, via an abbreviated *Twible* or any other means, is anathema." Well, OK then.

3: "Bishops should be married to one wife." Just so we've clarified that little matter. Otherwise, the Pastor seems to think polygamy's FINE.

4: "Don't let anyone give you any crap because you're young, Tim. Just give 'em crap right back because they're old."

5: "Don't help any young widows; they're all Satan-loving sluts. When they get old you can help them, if they survived your neglect."

6: "The love of money is the root of all evil." (P.S. Order *Love of Money* today at Amazon.com and get free shipping!)

WIDOW WELFARE ENROLLMENT

Qualifications for financial support:
- ☐ Over age 60
- ☐ Married only once
- ☐ Famous for good works
- ☐ Raised children
- ☐ Showed hospitality
- ☐ Washed the feet of the saints
- ☐ Helped the afflicted
- ☐ Did good in every way

(Young widows need not apply.)

Paul and "Paul"

In the ancient world, it was commonplace to write something in the style of another person or in honor of that person. It's like a form of reverse plagiarism—you write your piece but give someone else the credit for it.

We've come to the point in the New Testament when we start to see letters that are attributed to Paul but are unlikely to have been written by Paul. These are called the "pastoral epistles" or the "deutero-Pauline letters," depending on the extent of the speaker's overeducation and desire to impress you. Sometimes the author of these letters is referred to as "the Pastor" because he (and judging from how rigidly these letters interpret women's roles, in contrast to the original Paul's more freewheeling egalitarianism, it most likely was a "he") is very concerned about improving the situation for the turn-of-the-century Christian church.

So here's a summary of how the thirteen letters shake down in terms of probable authorship:

Definitely written by Paul: Romans, 1 and 2 Corinthians, Galatians, Philippians, Philemon, and 1 Thessalonians
Possibly written by Paul: Colossians and Ephesians
Probably not written by Paul: 2 Thessalonians
Definitely not written by Paul: 1 and 2 Timothy, Titus

So why do most scholars remove those last four letters from the Pauline canon? Some of the reasons are linguistic; those letters use different language than Paul's undisputed ones. But they also presuppose a later historical situation than Paul's in the 50s—one more consistent with what we know of the Christian church many decades later.

- Whereas Paul enjoyed a loose confederation of "fellow workers" in the gospel, the Pastoral Epistles have a full-blown church hierarchy with bishops, deacons, and grand poobahs.
- While Paul spoke often of the tension in the earliest churches between those who wanted to continue observing Judaism (like Peter) and those who thought it was no longer necessary (like Paul himself), in the Pastoral Epistles the question just doesn't come up, which would be consistent with an audience several generations removed from Judaism.
- Paul's belief that the appointed time of Jesus' return is probably tomorrow, or at the latest 9:00 next Tuesday, has been muted considerably in the Pastoral Epistles. 2 Thessalonians, in fact, is consumed with telling people *not* to expect the Lord's return anytime soon.
- Unlike Paul's uncontested letters, which were clearly directed to specific congregations and dealt with particular issues that had cropped up in those communities, the Pastoral Epistles have a more generic and less situational vibe.
- Paul's authority is never questioned in the Pastoral Epistles. Considering that in his other writings he was constantly defending his status as a legitimate apostle to people who challenged his position, this sudden respect is odd unless the letters are dated later, after Paul's martyrdom, when he's become Paul of Blessed Memory.

2 TIMOTHY

Overview: Paul's last will and testament allegedly left Little Timmy in charge, but leading the church is like herding cats.

1: Letter praises Tim's mom and grandma, who raised him. At least the Pastoral Epistles have *something* good to say about women.

2: Don't get sucked into stupid spats about religion. In other words, never read the comments on your blog posts.

3: "Every part of Scripture is God-breathed." So be sure to kill some unbelievers today! And a witch or two. The Bible says so.

4: "Fight the good fight! Finish the race! P.S. can you please bring my coat when you come? I accidentally left it in Troas. Xxoo."

Timothy discovers that leading the church is like herding cats.

TITUS

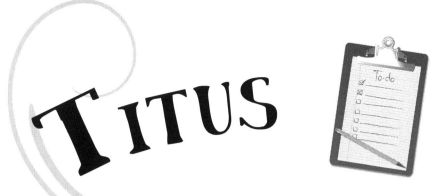

Overview: A dull, but mercifully short, sequel to 1 and 2 Timothy. You can basically skip this part unless you're an overachiever.

1: Grants biblical license to duct-tape the mouth of any Christian who rejects your (100% true) ideas. Hmm. I have some candidates.

2: "Older women, teach the younger women to obey their husbands. Keep busy at home. Knit something. And do shut up already."

3: "Folks, stop asking silly questions. Obey the government. Get over your massive addiction to Ancestry.com."

PHILEMON

Overview: Only NT letter directed to a single person and not a church. So you're reading someone else's mail, y'all.

1: "Hi, Phil! Paul here, returning your slave. (Subtext: Let him go.) Sorry to bug you. (Subtext: Let him go.) Love ya. TTYL."

Hebrews

Overview: You don't have to be circumcised to follow Jesus, but matzoh ball soup is always a good idea. Also, Jesus is like Supermoses.

1: "Jesus is G's Son and hangs out at his right hand. Angels, by contrast, are just jacked-up servants with wings." JC 5, Angels 0.

2: Jesus had to become fully human in order to understand just how much your life really sucks. But now he gets it.

3: "*¿Quién es más macho,* Jesus or Moses?" According to Hebrews, Jesus had more chest hair. He was G's Son, not just a servant. *Muy macho.*

4: The word of G is alive and active, and sharper than a double-edged sword. It also makes julienne fries.

5: High priest must possess empathy, be sinless, and suffer death. But the job security is unmatched: "You will be a priest forever."

6: "If you see G's light but turn it off, the power will be out forever and it'll be ALL YOUR FAULT." #demotivationalBibleverses

7: Jesus is the new Melchizedek. This 2.0 version is a permanent upgrade! Also, Jesus' name is a whole lot easier to spell.

8: Plan B: This time G will write his covenant in your heart, like when Mom used to sew mittens into the sleeves of your coat. Foolproof.

9: "Jesus is the new sacrifice." This is good news for us, but especially for lambs and goats, who bleat a collective sigh of relief.

10: "JC's sacrifice was once and for all time." G works hard to improve company efficiency. Next up: middle management priestly layoffs.

The "great cloud of witnesses"

11: All the superheroes of the OT, gathered in one place to whup ass! It's Old Home Week for Noah, Enoch, and Abraham. So good to see ya.

12: G disciplines his children. So if you're suffering, it means you're his legitimate offspring. There's a silver lining for you.

13: In closing: We know you're persecuted, but it's an honor. Truly. Just remember that when you're being impaled.

JAMES

Overview: Paul: "Grace rocks!" James: "Not so fast. Faith without works is DOA." And . . . we're still arguing two thousand years later.

1: Advice to bloggers and talk show hosts: Be quick to hear and slow to speak or get angry. Ask G for wisdom. *Then* open your fool mouth.

2: EPIC FAIL RELIGION: when a cold, hungry guy hears a Christian say, "Stay warm and be fed, pal!" while passing him by.

3: Smokey the Bear says, "Remember. Only you can prevent verbal forest fires. So please watch your tongue, or I will eat you."

4: Human beings are spoiled brats who crave power and kill for our various lusts. In other words, it's Henry VIII all over again.

5: The prayer of a righteous person is effective. So if your prayer's not answered, that means . . . but who's pointing fingers?

EPIC FAIL RELIGION

I PETER

Overview: Allegedly written by Peter to soothe persecuted Christians. But he was gone by then, having been persecuted to death himself.

1: "Hard times have tested your faith, but I see you're all still doing the Happy Dance. Gold star for attitude, people! Mad props!"

2: "Slaves, submit. Just Suck. It. Up. If your master's harsh, you'll get bonus points someday from the Great Overseer in the sky."

3: "Wives: see slave section in previous chapter. Submission's the name of the game. Also, ladies, please stop shopping at DeBeers."

4: "As Christians, you'll be insulted and whipped. This suffering makes you like Jesus, so it's every kind of awesome! Enjoy."

5: "Red alert. The enemy prowls about like a roaring lion waiting to devour you." Well, *hakuna matata* to you too.

2 PETER

Overview: "Beware of false teachers. Of which I am not one, just so we're clear. Those jerks are gonna ROAST IN HELL."

True Teachers	False Teachers
Peter	Bob the Prophet
Peter	Your Mom
Peter	 Everyone Else in the World

1: "I was with JC when he was transfigured. I heard G's voice! So I have serious street cred. Er, mountaintop cred."

2: "Pete" delineates some of the highly satisfying payback that'll happen to false teachers. We clearly touched a nerve there.

3: "P.S. JC met Dory en route to his Second Coming. She is a known Delayfish, so his return could take longer than expected."

L_ve
_ne
an_t_er

1 John ♥

Overview: All you need is love. All you need is love. All you need is love, love. Love is all you need. (And, of course, Jesus. Same diff.)

1: "If we say we don't sin, we deceive ourselves." This stinks, because self-deception feels much easier than the alternative.

2: How to recognize Antichrists: They'll deny G and JC. Also, sometimes their heads will spin 360 degrees. That is often a clue.

3: "Love one another; obey the commandments; don't hate." The Bible would be so much more succinct if we'd done all this the first time.

4: "Everyone who loves is born of G and knows G." Yeah, it's true. The Bible stole that idea from the final scene of *Les Miz*.

5: "To love G and G's children means to keep the commandments." You have to admire the simplicity of it, really.

2 JOHN ♥

Overview: John dashes off a quick note but then says he'd rather talk in person. He could have done both with an iPad.

1: Once more for the hearing impaired: LOVE one another. In case you missed the flaming all caps before: Just. LOVE.

3 JOHN ♥

Overview: John tells his BFF that hospitality to travelers is the work of G. And by coincidence, John will be in town soon! Hint hint.

1: When you provide guests with meals and a bed, you're serving G. So please make me chicken soup and a nice grilled cheese sandwich, OK?

JUDE

Overview: Red alert! Infiltrators slipped into your church and are posing as Christians. Beware of false prophets wearing WWJD bracelets.

1: Hey, Jude. Don't be afraid. You were made to cast out the sinners. The minute you let 'em into your church, then they'll besmirch . . .

REVELATION

Overview: The book Luther wanted out of the canon. The book that is not actually plural. Hello, Armageddpocalypse.

1: The visions in this book might suggest it's John the Revelator's extra-long LSD trip, but it was all OK'd by an angel. So cool your jets.

2: G takes four churches to task with a helpful mix of censure and praise. He's improved his people management skills since the OT.

3: JC: "Yoo hoo, here I am! I stand at the door and knock. Hey, is that fried chicken I smell? Let me in and we can hang out."

4: JC props the door open so JnRev can see heaven. It turns out heaven's more like glitzy Vegas than Iowa. This is good to know.

5: A hundred million angels say JC the Lamb is worthy of praise. For what it's worth, they have also endorsed him on LinkedIn.

WTF Is Revelation?

If there were an award for Weirdest Book of the Bible, Revelation would clobber its lesser rivals Ezekiel and Daniel 666 times over. Angels attacking humankind? Seven-headed dragons? A Great Whore of Babylon?

This is strange stuff. Despite the prevalence of people claiming to know exactly what Revelation means—who the Antichrist is, when Jesus is coming back—there's far more that we don't understand about it than we do. Revelation is not a conventional history or even much of a story at all; New Testament scholar Elaine Pagels says it "offers only visions—dreams and nightmares," making it obscure and difficult to interpret. Seth Rogen wasn't far off when, in publicizing his 2013 post-Rapture comedy *This Is the End*, he told NPR's *Fresh Air* that he found the Book of Revelation "crazy" and "unbelievable." As his writing partner Evan Goldberg put it, "*Lord of the Rings* got nothin' on this."

Here's what we do know about Revelation. The book is called Revelation, singular, and not Revelations, plural, because it was one long vision given to one lone person, John of Patmos. This John is not the "beloved disciple" of the Gospel of John or the Letters of John, unless that disciple lived an extremely long time and took a whole mess of drugs in the intervening decades—drugs that resulted in puzzling hallucinations and the near-total destruction of his earlier fluency in Greek. Revelation was probably written near the end of the first century, in the 90s CE, when many Christians were facing persecution at the hands of the Romans.

Pagels says that Revelation "barely squeezed into the canon to become the final book in the New Testament," not finding its place in Scripture until the bishop Athanasius was able to reinterpret Revelation's Enemy du Jour in the early fourth century. Athanasius taught that the great cosmic evil was not the Roman Empire, as had long been assumed (an interpretation that had become mighty inconvenient the moment the Roman emperor had converted to Christianity) and was instead heretical, uppity Christians.

But even then Revelation's place in the canon wasn't always secure. More than a thousand years later, Reformer Martin Luther argued to remove Revelation from the Bible because it was not overtly about Christ. He changed his mind when he began to see all the nifty ways he could use the book against the Catholic Church, which he soon branded as the Whore of Babylon. Luther was hardly the last religious leader to mine Revelation's bizarre apocalyptic imagery for useful ammunition in identifying his enemies as Antichrist.

But what does the book mean for us today? In the end, after the avenging angels have all worn themselves out with global destruction and the weary survivors of the war in heaven have tossed Satan into a pit, Revelation becomes a book about hope. (I know, I know, it doesn't sound like it. That's why it's important to stick with the book until the final chapter.) The new heaven and the new earth glimpsed by John of Patmos and recorded in this mondo-bizarro vision will feature no more death, no more sorrow or crying. God will dwell with the people in peace.

The Book of Revelation, and therefore the entire Bible, concludes with a beautiful foray back to a primordial garden, back to Genesis 1 (well, Genesis 2, but let's not be too picky here). Whereas once upon a time in Eden it was fruit that got humanity in trouble with God, now there will be abundant fruit trees of twelve varieties lining the banks of the river of life. Nothing accursed will be found there; there will be no night; neither will there be any sun because the presence of the Lord will shine a light for all. And God will reign forever. What's not hopeful about that?

6: JC opens a scroll, unleashing a can of whupass, and G starts pouring out judgment on nations. Uh, can we roll that scroll right back up?

7: Only 144,000 are saved. Statistically, the chance you'll be in this group is negligible, so don't break out the white robe just yet.

8: When seven angels start blowing their seven trumpets, human beings wish they had never, ever been touched by an angel.

9: The angelic destruction continues. They are enjoying human obliteration way too much. Very creative little terrorists, angels.

10: A kickass warrior angel has John eat a scroll that gives him wicked heartburn. Mom always SAID not to eat the Bible.

11: When the seventh angel opens G's temple in heaven, it's just like *Raiders of the Lost Ark*. You might want to close your eyes for this.

12: A sparkly woman gives birth to baby Jesus with a killer dragon as midwife. This could really spice up the nativity crèche at Christmas.

13: Killer dragon teams up with a beast marked with the number 666. I think the beast is actually Elmo. I'm keeping my eyes on him for sure.

14: G is trampling out the vintage where the grapes of wrath are stored. The problem is that WE are the grapes of wrath. Uh oh.

The Woman Clothed with the Sun
checks into the Labor & Delivery room.

 REVELATION **287**

15: Cue seven more angels, this time with "seven disasters." You've got to be kidding me. How can anyone still be alive on earth to destroy?

16: Each angel has a bowl with which to pour out disaster: fire, blood, hail, etc. Plus my favorite: frog-demons. Those are the funnest.

17: The Great Whore of Babylon rides a beast with seven heads and ten horns, each representing a king. And those kings are going DOWN.

18: Babylon's destroyed in just one hour, like a millstone sunk into the sea. Heaven rejoices! Babylon's partners in crime, not so much.

19: Time for the Wedding Supper of the Lamb. Just so we're clear, Jesus the lamb is not what's on the menu. It's kind of a metaphor.

20: Satan's bound for 1,000 years, then hurled into the Lake of Fire and Brimstone for 24/7 torment. Just deserts! Er, desserts. Whatever.

21: The following jobs will be obsolete in the new heaven and new earth: undertaker, grief therapist, and anesthesiologist. Awesome.

22: Bible ends with G opening a fruit-of-the-month club and restoring Eden. All has come full circle. (Warning: Do not add to story. Amen.)

The Seven Seals of Revelation

Notes: Or, Where to Find
What All the Smart People Said

Introduction

Unless otherwise marked, all non-*Twible* biblical quotations in this book are from the New Revised Standard Version.

Statistics on biblical literacy—or, more accurately, illiteracy—can be found in Stephen Prothero, *Religious Literacy: What Every American Needs to Know—and Doesn't* (San Francisco: HarperOne, 2009), Kindle locations 224, 465, 586, 595, and 602.

Genesis

God's Plan B: Richard Elliott Friedman, *Commentary on the Torah with a New English Translation* (San Francisco: HarperSanFrancisco, 2001), 49.

Exodus

Did the Exodus really happen?: Michael Coogan, *The Old Testament: A Very Short Introduction* (New York: Oxford University Press, 2008), 47.

Is God trustworthy? Debbie Blue, *Consider the Birds: A Provocative Guide to the Bible* (Nashville, TN: Abingdon Press, 2013), 51.

Argumentative conversations with God: Avivah Gottlieb Zornberg, *The Particulars of Rapture: Reflections on Exodus* (New York: Doubleday, 2001), 415–418.

Leviticus

Do sweat the small stuff: Kathleen Norris, *The Quotidian Mysteries: Laundry, Liturgy, and "Women's Work"* (Mahwah, NJ: Paulist Press, 1998), 21–22.

Deuteronomy

It's the economy, stupid: Walter Brueggemann, *Journey to the Common Good* (Louisville, KY: Westminster John Knox Press, 2010), 39.

Joshua

A golden age. Or not: Gregory Mobley, "Joshua," *Theological Bible Commentary*, edited by Gail R. O'Day and David L. Petersen (Louisville, KY: Westminster John Knox Press, 2009), 77–86.

Judges

The crappiest king: John Kaltner, Steven McKenzie, and Joel Kilpatrick, *The Uncensored Bible: The Bawdy and Naughty Bits of the Good Book* (San Francisco: HarperOne, 2008), 59–62.

Text of terror: See Phyllis Trible, *Texts of Terror: Literary-Feminist Readings of Biblical Narratives* (Philadelphia: Fortress Press, 1984).

Ruth

Did she or didn't she?: Joan Chittister, *The Story of Ruth: Twelve Moments in Every Woman's Life* (Grand Rapids, MI: Eerdmans, 2000), 76–78.

2 Samuel

And you thought your family was messed up?: One complication of this fairy tale is that Solomon wasn't really the fifth son of David, but somewhat further down the line. In fact, he wasn't even the oldest surviving son of the relationship between David and Bathsheba. But the Bible has little to say about Solomon's full brothers, or why he was the only one from his nuclear family to go toe-to-toe with his older half-brothers for the throne. Clearly, Bathsheba saw some strong leadership potential in this son, and David either agreed with her or was too far gone by that point to argue.

1 Kings
Inside Solomon's temple: For more on the temple, see John Goldingay, *1 & 2 Kings for Everyone* (Louisville, KY: Westminster John Knox Press, 2011), 27–33. For Eugene Peterson's translation, see *The Message Study Bible: Capturing the Notes and Reflections of Eugene H. Peterson* (Colorado Springs: NavPress, 2012), 612.

2 Kings
10 biblical names that shouldn't be used again anytime soon: For biblical names, see the *Holman Bible Dictionary* at http://www.studylight.org/dic/hbd/.

1 Chronicles
What's missing from the David story?: For more on Saul's suicide, see Alejandro Botta, "1 Chronicles," in *The New Interpreter's Bible One-Volume Commentary*, edited by Beverly Roberts Gaventa and David Petersen (Nashville: Abingdon Press, 2010), 244.

2 Chronicles
Inside Solomon's temple: See John Goldingay, *1 & 2 Kings for Everyone* (Louisville, KY: Westminster John Knox Press, 2011), 26–29; and Eugene Peterson, *The Message Study Bible: Capturing the Notes and Reflections of Eugene H. Peterson* (Colorado Springs, CO: 2012), 612.

Nehemiah
A slow rebuilding: Mark Throntweit, *Ezra-Nehemiah*, Interpretation series (Louisville, KY: Westminster John Knox Press, 1992), 16. John Goldingay, *Ezra, Nehemiah & Esther for Everyone* (Louisville, KY: Westminster John Knox Press, 2012), 3–7, 106–109, 123–124.

Job
The friends of Job: Mark Larrimore, *The Book of Job: A Biography* (Princeton, NJ: Princeton University Press, 2013), 22–23, 242.

Psalms

The full spectrum of human emotion: Kathleen Norris, *The Psalms* (New York: Riverhead Books, 1997), ix.

Who wrote the Psalms?: Robert Alter, *The Book of Psalms: A Translation with Commentary* (New York: W.W. Norton, 2007), xv.

The beauty of Psalm 88: Alter, 310.

The ABC Bible: See Alter, 419.

Dashing babies' heads against the rocks, and other Bible fun: Alter, 475.

Proverbs

The How-to Bible: Ellen F. Davis, *Proverbs, Ecclesiastes, and the Song of Songs* (Louisville, KY: Westminster John Knox Press, 2000), 11.

Five money rules from the Book of Proverbs: Davis, *Proverbs, Ecclesiastes, and the Song of Songs*, 21, 93–96, 116–119.

Strong woman: See Davis, *Proverbs, Ecclesiastes, and the Song of Songs*, 152–155. The occurrences of the word *chayil/hayil* in the Hebrew Bible are discussed at http://www.biblestudytools.com/lexicons/hebrew/kjv/chayil.html. The word and its translation are discussed in Kathleen Farmer, *Who Knows What is Good? A Commentary on the Books of Proverbs and Ecclesiastes* (Grand Rapids, Michigan: Wm. B. Eerdmans Publishing, 1991), 124. See also Jana Riess, "The Woman of Worth: Impressions of Proverbs 31:10–31," *Dialogue: A Journal of Mormon Thought Spring* 1997 30(1): 141-151, available online at http://www.dialoguejournal.com/wp-content/uploads/sbi/articles/Dialogue_V30N01_147.pdf. And the absolutely awful quotation is from Robina and John Wakeford, *In Praise of Women* (New York: Harper & Row, 1980).

Isaiah

Three different Isaiahs?: Gerald T. Sheppard, "Isaiah," *The HarperCollins Bible Commentary*, Revised Edition, edited by James L. Mays (San Francisco: HarperSanFrancisco, 2000), 489–492.

Have a little faith: Walter Brueggemann, *Isaiah* 1-39 (Louisville, KY: Westminster John Knox Press, 1998), 65–72.

On eagles' wings: Debbie Blue, *Consider the Birds,* 73–74.

Jeremiah

I know the plans I have for you: See R.E. Clements, *Jeremiah* (Louisville, KY: Westminster John Knox Press, 1988), 169–173.

Lamentations

Harvey Cox does the Lamentations section of the book he co-wrote with Stephanie Paulsell, *Lamentations and Song of Songs.* It's an outstanding commentary for ordinary people who aren't interested in the technical minutiae of biblical scholarship but just want to get to the heart of the matter. For example, he describes his evolving understanding of Lamentations in the context of having been an American soldier in Germany in 1946, when a defeated people had to come to terms with the extent of their sin and the terrible challenge of recovering from a devastation they had brought upon themselves. (Louisville, KY: Westminster John Knox Press, 2012), 3–167.

Ezekiel

Ezekiel bread: The website for Ezekiel 4:9 bread is found at foodforlife.com. For a funny modern perspective on Ezekiel bread (and many other topics related to the Bible), see AJ Jacobs, *The Year of Living Biblically* (New York: Simon & Schuster, 2007), 310.

The F word is in the Bible?!: John A. Goldingay, "Ezekiel," *Eerdmans Commentary on the Bible*, James D.G. Dunn, general editor (Grand Rapids, MI: Eerdmans, 2003), 635. See also Jacqueline Lapsley, "Ezekiel," *The New Interpreters' Bible One-Volume Commentary*, Beverly Gaventa and David L. Petersen, general editors (Nashville: Abingdon Press, 2010), 463.

Don't trust anyone under thirty: See Daniel Bodi, *The Book of Ezekiel and the Poem of Erra* (Orbis Biblicus et Orientalis) (Vandenhoeck & Ruprecht, 1991), 11–12. Bodi writes that "the book of Ezekiel contains serious theological problems which had already troubled the ancient rabbis. On this account the public reading and even the private study of Ezekiel was restricted. Ezekiel 1 was for some time banned as a *haftorah* reading in the liturgy . . . . A minimum age limit of thirty was set for its study, and restrictions were imposed even on class size."

Matthew
The Christmas story: Timothy Beal, *Biblical Literacy: The Essential Bible Stories Everyone Needs to Know* (San Francisco: HarperOne, 2009), 197–198.

The sheep and the goats: See www.m25m.org for more information on Matthew 25 Ministries.

Mark
The beta version of Mark: Reynolds Price, *Three Gospels* (New York: Simon & Schuster Touchstone, 1996), 59.

Luke
The gospel of the margins: N.T. Wright, *Luke for Everyone* (Cambridge, UK: SPCK, 2001), 47–49.

The Pharisees: Steve Mason, "Pharisees," *The Eerdmans Dictionary of the Bible*, edited by David Noel Freedman (Grand Rapids, MI: Eerdmans, 2000), 1043–1044.

John

What kind of love?: Mark A. Matson, *John* Interpretation Bible Studies (Louisville, KY: Westminster John Knox Press, 2002), 126.

Acts

Know the Book of Acts: The answers are: 1 (B); 2 (A); 3 (C); 4 (C); and 5 (B). If you got all five right, congratulations! Great will your reward be in heaven. If you did *not* get all give correct, don't sweat. Paul would say that you are saved by grace, not by works.

1 Corinthians

The love chapter: N.T. Wright, *Paul for Everyone*: *1 Corinthians* (Cambridge: SPCK, 2003), 177.

1 Timothy

Paul and "Paul": J. Christian Beker, *Heirs of Paul: Paul's Legacy in the New Testament and in the Church Today* (Minneapolis, MN: Augsburg Fortress, 1991), esp. 36-47.

Revelation

WTF is Revelation?: Elaine Pagels, *Revelations: Visions, Prophecy, and Politics in the Book of Revelation* (New York: Viking, 2012) 1–3, 58–60, 134–142. Pagels sums up the book beautifully when she writes, "The Book of Revelation reads as if John had wrapped up all our worst fears—fears of violence, plague, wild animals, unimaginable horrors emerging from the abyss below the earth, lightning, thunder, hail, earthquakes, erupting volcanoes, and the atrocities of torture and war—into one gigantic nightmare. Yet instead of ending in total destruction, his visions finally open to the new Jerusalem—a glorious city filled with light. John's visions of dragons, monsters, mothers, and whores speak less to our head than to our heart: like nightmares and dreams, they speak to what we fear, and what we hope." Pagels, 171.

Who's Who in *The Twible*

Confused about the Bible's ginormous cast of characters? Here's a quick guide to some of them, focusing primarily on the ones whose real names are abbreviated for *The Twible*.

12: The 12 disciples of Jesus. Mostly clueless with a scattered chance of understanding.

Aar: Aaron, the brother of Moses and the founder of a whole priestly line. If Joshua is responsible for slaughtering the most people in the Bible (and this is a contested category, with many competitors), then Aaron wins the award for ritually slaughtering the most animals. He is not widely admired by vegan readers of the Bible.

Abs: Absalom, the rebellious son of King David. Well, the *most* rebellious son. They were none of them saints, you know.

Amos: A dresser of sycamore trees who moonlighted as a prophet. Apparently there wasn't enough of a market for clothed sycamore trees, so he had to supplement.

Bath: Bathsheba, who was seduced by King David after he glimpsed her taking a bath. Talk about a bad case of nominative determinism.

Dan: Daniel, a righteous Jewish teen who successfully faced down lions—and worse, the Babylonian court. He could read the writing on the wall.

Dave: King David. Despite the fact that he was an adulterer and a murderer, the sun basically shines out of his ass during the Books of Chronicles. That's charisma, baby.

Est: Queen Esther, who saved the Jewish people. Note that the Bible never actually claims she was an asparagus, like she is in the Veggie Tales version. The animators may have taken a few liberties.

Ezra: A reformer, priest, scribe, and builder who tried to put Jerusalem back together again more than a century after the Babylonians destroyed it. He was also the mayor in his two minutes of free time.

G: God. CEO and big enchilada. Diagnosed with multiple personality disorder, bipolar disorder, obsessive compulsive disorder, and intermittent explosive disorder. But we're still supposed to love him.

Hab: Habakkuk, a neglected prophet from the Hebrew Bible/Old Testament. It's sad that we ignore him nowadays, because his whole book is about how he felt God blew him off too.

Hag: The prophet Haggai, who was also something of a hag; another case of nominative determinism.

Ho: Hosea the prophet. Husband of Gomer, who was a prostitute. This was not a super-fun marriage for Hosea, who took it out on his kids by naming them "Not Pitied," "Jezreel," and "Not My People."

Isa: Isaiah the prophet, who was responsible for the first portion of the book of Isaiah. The other parts were written centuries later just to trick us.

JC: Jesus Christ, the Son of God. Even I can't find anything sarcastic to say about him, so let's move on.

Jer: Jeremiah, the gloom-and-doom prophet. If Zoloft had been available in the seventh century BCE, the Bible might have been a much more optimistic book overall.

JnBap: John the Baptist, who baptized Jesus in the Jordan River. Head sold separately. Locusts and honey also not included.

JnRev: John the Revelator, probable author of the trippy book of Revelation. Although he was arrested for suspected hallucinogenic possession, nothing was ever proven, so Revelation remained part of the New Testament canon.

Job: One of the only characters in *The Twible* who gets to keep his entire name, instead of having it shortened to accommodate Twitter. And that's a nice gesture, because Job loses every other freakin' thing.

John: John the Beloved Disciple. John calls himself "beloved" in his own gospel, though, so you can take the whole "I'm Jesus' favorite" schtick with a grain of salt.

Jon: Jonathan, Dave's BFF and the son of Dave's main rival and archenemy, King Saul. This story is recounted in the dictionary right next to the word *awkward*.

Josh: Joshua, Moses' chief military dude and jihadist, who conquered Jericho and a lot of other places in cold blood.

MM: Mary Magdalene, a follower of Jesus who was not a prostitute. Just so we're clear on that point.

Mary: Mary, the mother of Jesus. The Magnificat lady. Also not a prostitute, but probably not a perpetual virgin either. Last seen wearing blue.

MaryBeth: Mary of Bethany, sister of Lazarus and Martha. This Mary was the one learning at Jesus' feet while Martha washed all the dishes. Nice work if you can get it, MaryBeth.

Neh: Nehemiah. Although he was the cupbearer to the King of Persia and living far away from Jerusalem, Nehemiah's passion was all about rebuilding that destroyed city. Thanks to exemplary career counseling and LinkedIn connections, he relocated and reinvented himself as an engineer.

Paul: Formerly known as Saul. A onetime persecutor of Christians who became a Jesus freak, world traveler, and tireless letter-writer, even if his letters make you feel like you'll never please him.

Pete: Peter, Jesus' lead disciple who denied the Lord three times after the crucifixion but managed to turn himself around and prove his faithfulness in leading the early church. Note that Peter and Paul didn't always get along, even after they formed a folk music group with their friend Mary.

Phil: Philemon, a well-to-do leader in the Colossian house church. What Paul's short letter to him says about slavery is so ambivalent and hard to judge that both Northern abolitionists and Southern slaveholders used it to justify their positions. The Bible is nothing if not malleable.

Q: Qoheleth, the grumpy author of the Book of Ecclesiastes. He lamented that there was no end to the making of books, yet he went and wrote one. Around here we call that irony.

Rach: Rachel, the favorite wife of Jacob. After many years of begging God for a child, she became the mother of Joseph and then died giving birth to Benjamin. We hope the kids were worth it.

Sam: The prophet Samuel. When the people begged him for a king, Samuel warned them it would be disastrous. But did they listen? NO. And then when King Saul turned nasty they didn't even have the grace to let Samuel say, "I told you so." It's not easy being the prophet.

Sol: King Solomon. As ruthless, murderous, and lovable as Tony Soprano, but with about a thousand more wives and concubines. Dispensed great wisdom while oppressing and enslaving his own people. What can we say? Kings are complicated.

Zacc: Zacchaeus, the tax collector who scurried up a tree just to find a brand-new way to ask Jesus to dinner. Evite had not been invented yet.

Zech: Zechariah, the prophet of the Hebrew Bible/Old Testament. Not to be confused with Zechariah, John the Baptist's dad, who was struck dumb for his disbelief when an angel told him that his aged wife Elizabeth would bear a son. If you do confuse the two men, don't be alarmed if one of them gesticulates wildly but silently to communicate that you've got the wrong guy.

Zeke: Ezekiel, the prophet of the dry bones and other great stories. He didn't receive his prophetic call until the age of thirty, which should give you hope if you've gotten all the way through your twenties and feel you haven't accomplished much with your life.

Zeph: The prophet Zephaniah, who spoke out against religious corruption and moral decay during the reign of Josiah. The fact that God went ahead with plans for Jerusalem's destruction probably shows you how well the people listened to Zephaniah and changed their ways.

Acknowledgments

I have come to believe in my study of the Bible that one of the great sins of modern North American interpretation is our almost wholly individualistic way of approaching Scripture. The Bible is the story of several thousand years of community, not a pockmarked greatest hits book about a few remarkable individuals who can be extracted as our personal heroes.

Which is my long and roundabout way of saying that it takes a village to raise a book. That is especially true of a quirky project like *The Twible*, which could not have happened without a generous community of early readers. The book you're holding is the result of many conversations and four years of Twitter community-building. I will try to remember the readers who offered suggestions, but if I've forgotten anyone, please forgive me.

As the cartoonist, Leighton Connor enriched this project with his talent and wonderful sense of humor, and his art created some of the funniest moments in the book. It was a joy to work together. He wishes to thank Matt Kish for creative inspiration, Josh Burnett and Doug Meyer for encouragement, and Jeffrey Johnson for assisting with the dragon in the Book of Revelation. He would also like to thank his loving wife Alice for her unflagging support. You can visit his blog at comicsclassgo. blogspot.com and his web comic *Laser Brigade* at laserbrigade.thecomicseries.com.

Leighton is a member of my writing group, and he, along with my longtime friend Jamie Noyd, made untold revisions over the course of several years, most especially with the opening chapters of Acts. Many other people made suggestions throughout: Rosalynde Frandsen Welch helped cement the punchline of Proverbs 31, and Aaron Taylor made Mark 7 funnier. Genesis 6 was improved by a suggestion from Debra Rienstra; Ben Spackman gave me a reference for the meaning of skubalon in the writings of Paul; and Lil Copan and Chris and Christine Ferrebee helped me think about positioning the book as a whole. The Theologigglers came up with sidebar ideas for me to incorporate into the book revisions.

I had a more formal core group of readers as I reworked *The Twible* for publication, and all of them deserve much more than mere thanks and a free copy of the book. They are: Marcy Bain, Elise Erikson Barrett, Brent Bill, Andrew Burnett, Dawn Burnett, Kelly Hughes, Mark Kellner, Janet

Kincaid, Susan Elia MacNeal, Nick Mosca, Steven Peck, Zina Peterson, Karen Clark Ristine, Marion Saeternes, Brian Shope, Aaron Taylor, and David Zimmerman. Nancy Hopkins-Greene provided eagle-eye copy editing and terrific feedback in the final stages.

One of the best aspects of self-publishing—which in this case is more aptly termed "team publishing"—is that I was able to cherry pick the best people I have worked with on previous books. The excellent designers at Paraclete Press did the logo, cover design, and interior layout, meeting the challenges of this unusual project and crazy timeline with grace and professionalism. Many blog readers entered a contest to offer early feedback about the logo and cover design of the book, and I am grateful to all of them, and especially to LaVonne Neff and Ellen Painter Dollar, whose suggestions helped steer us in the right direction. Kelly Hughes of DeChant-Hughes & Associates did the publicity for this book because I knew after working with Kelly twice before that she was quite simply the best in the business. She has also become a cherished friend.

I'd be remiss if I didn't thank the fans who have been so supportive of this project and of my memoir, *Flunking Sainthood*. It was a challenge to write that book because of the vulnerability a memoir about failure requires; I was apprehensive about sending my personal and spiritual shortcomings out into the world. But instead of judgment, what readers have given me is cupful after overflowing cupful of grace; they have responded with their own stories of trying, and failing, and trying again. I am profoundly grateful to the people who risk sharing their stories with me, the churches that have invited me to speak, and to all of the readers who have taken a chance on my writing.

Finally, I want to thank my husband and daughter for their good humor and understanding about all the hours I've spent these last four years with my nose in a commentary. Phil has been a partner in every sense of the word, his calm sturdiness a rock for me in good times and bad. This project was going on during periods of intense emotional upheaval, including the deaths of both my parents. My mother's death in early 2013 after a very brief illness is one of the most painful things that has ever happened to me. She loved this bizarre little project and did not live to see its completion, so it is bittersweet to be publishing this without her sitting beside me at a book signing or giving a copy to every single person she knew. This book is dedicated to her in gratitude for her generosity of spirit and devotion to books. Somewhere, she is proud.

Twenty-five percent of author proceeds after expenses are being divided equally among the following five charities that provide humanitarian aid and disaster relief around the world:

- UNICEF (unicef.org)
- The LDS Humanitarian Aid Fund (ldscharities.org)
- Heifer International (heifer.org)
- Episcopal Relief and Development (episcopalrelief.org)
- Matthew 25 Ministries (m25m.org)

It is my hope that this book can bring laughter to readers as well as tangible help to people in need. There aren't too many things I am completely certain about where the Bible is concerned, but one of my rock-solid convictions is this: The Bible makes it clear that we are all God's children, and each of us has a part to play in ensuring that the kingdom of God is among us (Luke 17:21).

God bless you.

—Jana

Made in the USA
San Bernardino, CA
28 October 2013